The Patient
Revolution

Wiley & SAS Business Series

The Wiley & SAS Business Series presents books that help senior-level managers with their critical management decisions.

Titles in the Wiley & SAS Business Series include:

Agile by Design: An Implementation Guide to Analytic Lifecycle Management by Rachel Alt-Simmons

Analytics in a Big Data World: The Essential Guide to Data Science and Its Applications by Bart Baesens

Bank Fraud: Using Technology to Combat Losses by Revathi Subramanian

Big Data Analytics: Turning Big Data into Big Money by Frank Ohlhorst

Big Data, Big Innovation: Enabling Competitive Differentiation through Business Analytics by Evan Stubbs

Business Analytics for Customer Intelligence by Gert Laursen

Business Intelligence Applied: Implementing an Effective Information and Communications Technology Infrastructure by Michael Gendron

Business Intelligence and the Cloud: Strategic Implementation Guide by Michael S. Gendron

Business Transformation: A Roadmap for Maximizing Organizational Insights by Aiman Zeid

Connecting Organizational Silos: Taking Knowledge Flow Management to the Next Level with Social Media by Frank Leistner

Data-Driven Healthcare: How Analytics and BI Are Transforming the Industry by Laura Madsen

Delivering Business Analytics: Practical Guidelines for Best Practice by Evan Stubbs

Demand-Driven Forecasting: A Structured Approach to Forecasting, Second Edition by Charles Chase

Demand-Driven Inventory Optimization and Replenishment: Creating a More Efficient Supply Chain by Robert A. Davis

Developing Human Capital: Using Analytics to Plan and Optimize Your Learning and Development Investments by Gene Pease, Barbara Beresford, and Lew Walker

The Executive's Guide to Enterprise Social Media Strategy: How Social Networks Are Radically Transforming Your Business by David Thomas and Mike Barlow

Economic and Business Forecasting: Analyzing and Interpreting Econometric Results by John Silvia, Azhar Iqbal, Kaylyn Swankoski, Sarah Watt, and Sam Bullard

Financial Institution Advantage and the Optimization of Information Processing by Sean C. Keenan

Financial Risk Management: Applications in Market, Credit, Asset, and Liability Management and Firmwide Risk by Jimmy Skoglund and Wei Chen

Foreign Currency Financial Reporting from Euros to Yen to Yuan: A Guide to Fundamental Concepts and Practical Applications by Robert Rowan

For more information on any of the above titles, please visit www.wiley.com.

The Patient Revolution

How Big Data and Analytics Are Transforming the Healthcare Experience

Krisa Tailor

Published by John Wiley & Sons, Inc., Hoboken, New Jersey.

Published simultaneously in Canada.

For general information on our other products and services or for technical support, please contact our Customer Care Department within the United States at (800) 762-2974, outside the United States at (317) 572-3993 or fax (317) 572-4002.

Wiley publishes in a variety of print and electronic formats and by print-on-demand. Some material included with standard print versions of this book may not be included in e-books or in print-on-demand. If this book refers to media such as a CD or DVD that is not included in the version you purchased, you may download this material at http://booksupport.wiley.com. For more information about Wiley products, visit www.wiley.com.

Library of Congress Cataloging-in-Publication Data:

Names: Tailor, Krisa, 1986-
Title: The patient revolution : how big data and analytics are transforming the health care experience / Krisa Tailor.
Description: 1 | Hoboken, New Jersey : John Wiley & Sons, Inc., [2016] | Series: Wiley & SAS business series | Includes index.
Identifiers: LCCN 2015035915| ISBN 9781119130000 (hardcover) | ISBN 9781119130178 (ePDF) | ISBN 9781119130185 (ePub)
Subjects: LCSH: Medical care–Technological innovations. | Medical innovations. | Medical technology–Management. | BISAC: COMPUTERS / Database Management / Data Mining.
Classification: LCC R855.3 .T35 2015 | DDC 610.285–dc23 LC record available at http://lccn.loc.gov/2015035915

Cover Design: Wiley
Cover Image: Healthcare Icons © iStock.com / VICTOR

Printed in the United States of America

10 9 8 7 6 5 4 3 2 1

To Jim Goodnight

Contents

Preface

Our healthcare system may be broken, but the opportunities to fix it are abundant. That's why I embarked on a remarkably exciting journey to write this book. Writing a book about healthcare, though, is just as overwhelming as it is exciting. On one hand, we have some of the biggest transformations happening today across the industry, and on the other hand, there are a growing number of questions about how to change. It's without doubt that the path to healthcare innovation is filled with unknowns.

However, I'm hopeful that by leading with empathy and by empowering the patient, we can change how healthcare works. I envision a newly designed system that's focused on both sickness and wellness, in which health is seamlessly integrated into our daily lives, and where care is so uniquely personalized that no two people are provided identical treatments.

This shift will happen by taking healthcare into the experience economy, where patients are now consumers and consumers are active participants in their healthcare. The new health economy is about the totality of health, not the occasional encounters with the system that we're used to. Unique service experiences are crafted for each individual, and they stretch well beyond the four walls of a doctor's office. They consider every element across people, process, and place, and through an unwavering consistency in delivering value, these experiences result in more engaged healthcare consumers.

Data and analytics are what will power the new health economy, and with their use, technology will become so powerful that we won't even notice it's there. Just imagine receiving a custom recommendation from your wearable device on what to order as you walk into a new restaurant. Little do you know that it's information like your health goals, historic calorie counts, food preferences, and location, all working with analytics and millions of other data points behind the scenes, to give you the information you need at exactly the right time. Or, imagine if you were a clinician and could receive personalized diagnoses and proposed interventions automatically within your patients' health records. Analytics would transform unimaginable amounts of data, like doctors' notes, lab tests, and medical imaging on millions of individuals, to create personalized and optimal recommendations.

These are some of the ideas about next-generation healthcare that I sought to shed light on in this book. I love to explore the intersection of healthcare, technology, and human-centered design, and bringing together these three areas, which I'm so passionate about, is what made this book-writing journey special for me.

My hope is that you expand your thinking of the possibilities of technology and data in healthcare, and that you are encouraged to innovate through a lens of human-centeredness. Whether it's new healthcare products, services, or policies that we're creating, if we focus on the needs of individuals and meeting them wherever they may be in their health journey, we'll reach our healthcare system's ultimate goal of keeping people healthy.

Acknowledgments

There are many individuals who have inspired and supported me in my career and book-writing journey, a few of whom I'd like to mention.

First, I'd like to thank Dr. Jim Goodnight, CEO of SAS, for both believing in me and investing in me. I would not have been where I am in my career without your support.

In 2013, I was given the opportunity to work in SAS's Health and Life Sciences Global Practice, to develop and manage a new healthcare product. I am grateful to all the individuals who collaborated with me on this work, including Bryan Engle, Matt Gross, and Deidra Peacock. Further, I'm fortunate to work with the amazing individuals on my team who are passionate about what they do and who inspire the people around them, including Patrick Homer, Dr. Mark Wolff, and Laurie Rose. Additionally, I'd like to thank my friend and colleague, Dr. Graham Hughes, for his insights and mentorship over the last several years.

My passion for healthcare innovation and design thinking grew tremendously after working with DXLab, and I'd like to thank CEO Lance Cassidy for being a constant source of inspiration, for providing an excerpt for the book, and for his creative guidance. I'm grateful to the entire DXLab team, including Lance, Engin Kapkin, and Matt Bell, for their work on the mind map and experience blueprint.

Finally, I'd like to thank my family—my mom, my dad, and my sisters, Tina and Sunaina—for their unwavering love and support.

About the Author

Krisa Tailor is a Global Industry Consultant in SAS's Health & Life Sciences Global Practice, where she helps healthcare organizations worldwide to address today's most pressing healthcare issues. She joined SAS in 2008, and has since then worked across a variety of areas within healthcare, including policy, product management, and consulting. She is also the CEO and co-founder of Remedy—a digital health platform for managing chronic pain (remedymypain.com).

Krisa is passionate about next-generation healthcare products and services, health analytics, digital health, and design thinking. You can read her insights about these topics and others on her social media and her blog.

Twitter: @krisatailor

Blog: blogs.sas.com/content/hls/author/krisatailor

LinkedIn: linkedin.com/in/krisatailor

The Patient
Revolution

PART I

Think

CHAPTER **1**

Introduction

PAIN POINTS

One thing that many of us SAS employees have in common, aside from our love for free M&M's and Zumba class at lunch, is something a little less glamorous. It's unfortunately pain: back pain, shoulder pain, neck pain, you name it. But it isn't unique to SAS. Many corporations, especially large software companies like us, share the same challenge. With over 5,000 people on our Cary, NC, campus, we definitely have our fair share of hunched-over-their-computer-screen employees.

Don't take me wrong, though; SAS isn't one of Fortune's top places to work for nothing. While we have world-class healthcare, a wonderful fitness center, and an ergonomics department all onsite, we, however, can't escape the fact that some jobs require long periods of sitting. Well, it turns out that sitting is really bad for you and can evolve into some serious chronic pain. And unfortunately, the M&M's don't relieve pain.

Chronic pain has become so widespread that one out of three Americans suffers from it and it costs our nation over $600 billion a year, which is more than the yearly costs for cancer, heart disease, and diabetes.[1] That's probably the least alarming statistic. Lower back pain, for example, affects 80 percent of the adult population and is the number-one cause of lost workdays in the United States.[2] And often, that's just the beginning of the vicious pain cycle; chronic pain can lead to obesity and chronic diseases such as diabetes, and to injuries and employment disabilities, not to mention the loss of productivity and costs to individuals and employers like SAS. But it's not just the adult population who's in pain. Have you ever heard of "text neck"? The younger generations—whose lives revolve around mobile and tech—are experiencing pain as young as in their teenage years; so much so that it's estimated that 25 percent of today's young adults will become disabled before they retire.[3]

Pain is tricky and confusing in so many ways, which makes it a really difficult problem to tackle. It can fluctuate a lot in intensity, occur in multiple places at once, and it doesn't always appear where the problem originates from. It really doesn't help solve the mystery when the pain in your right knee is contributing to a problem in your left gluteus. (Yes, that's how strange it is.) In a nutshell, it's a hard thing to get to the bottom of. Listening to so many pain stories over the years, I found that people often accept pain as a regular part of their lives. There was my friend Leigh, who was visiting a chiropractor biweekly for five years straight—it was a part of his Friday routine; my colleague John, who was in so much pain for two years that he one day found himself lying on his office floor unable to get up; and Melissa, whose lower back pain that she kept avoiding eventually led to severe knee pain. And there was my own experience in which my long nights of sitting (thank you, grad school) led to pain all over my right side. It was beyond physical, though; the emotional toll it took on all of us was draining. Managing the consequences of pain was tough. Tracking it was tough. Finding a solution was tough. I really wanted to do something about it.

Sometime last year I had an idea that could possibly help people manage their pain better. And after seeing some of the outrageous statistics, I was convinced that there was a way to curb *some* of the $600 billion in costs. So about 30 seconds after my brainwave moment (I admit I briefly felt as if I'd solved all the world's problems), I called my friend Lance, who's the CEO of DXLab—a local design consultancy that creates remarkable products and services. Following an hour-long phone conversation about the pains of pain, Lance and I mapped out a plan for incubating my idea and we were on our way.

BIRTH OF A START-UP

Lance and his team at DXLab use a process called *design thinking* to take ideas to implementation in a short period of time. Design thinking is a human-centered approach to innovation that translates observations into insights and insights into products and services that improve lives.[4] I've been a fan of the methodology since I was introduced to it during my days at NC State University, because of the way it converges creativity with business innovation. Its emphasis on human needs is what drives the approach and is what makes it ideal for solving healthcare challenges.

The process that Lance described to me was simple and refreshing. It looked like Figure 1.1.

Design thinking is unique because it gets people involved from the get-go. The very first thing we'd do is customer discovery—to understand the real issues of managing pain from the *customer's* point of view,

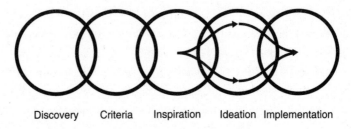

Discovery   Criteria   Inspiration   Ideation Implementation

Figure 1.1 Design Thinking Process

rather than *my* point of view. Is managing pain *really* a problem for people? Connecting with people and hearing their stories lets us gain empathy for the individuals, and also helps us define and validate our problems.

So that's what I did. Luckily, I had already expedited this step through many previous conversations around pain, but to put the structure I needed around it, I spoke with several individuals, through workshops and one-on-one interviews, to dive deeper into their pain stories and experiences. I wanted to understand both their obvious needs and their *latent* needs—needs that may be more difficult to articulate. But my customers weren't only those individuals experiencing pain. It was important to extend my understanding to their network of interactions and to hear how the issues affected them as well. So I connected with those who treat and manage pain; medical professionals such as physical therapists, pain medicine specialists, and chiropractors play an important role in the management of pain.

At the end of these conversations, I had defined and validated multiple problems from the patients' and the providers' points of view. It turned out that there were just as many problems on the provider side in managing pain as there were on the patient's side, and this shed light on what some of the barriers in pain management are. Most important, though, I gained a sense of *empathy* for both the patients and providers—the first and foundational component of human-centered design. It's something we don't do in healthcare as much as we should, even though we strive to be a patient-centric system. Taking this step before any discussion of the technology or design of the product was eye-opening and put me in a much better position to create something that met both the functional and emotional needs of individuals.

What I learned when I began to see the issues through their eyes was invaluable. I heard about many patient experiences, both good and bad (mostly bad), as they dealt with their pain. Some people had seen dozens of providers for their pain; some of them blamed their provider for their continuous pain; many were frustrated with trying to keep up with their evolving pain and trying to explain it to their providers; many thought they'd find a cure quicker if they weren't having to go from provider to provider to find the best treatment. And everyone said their pain might be healed quicker if the experience was better, more seamless, and easier. What they wanted was meaningful conversations, to get more value out of their doctor's visit, to share their pain story more effectively, and most important, to find a remedy to their pain. One thing was absolutely certain—managing pain needed to be a better experience.

A huge untapped market began to take shape before my eyes, and thus, Remedy was born.

EXPERIENCE IS THE TEACHER OF ALL THINGS

About a year ago, I finally got around to reading *Change by Design*, by Tim Brown, CEO and president of the highly talented design firm IDEO. The book had been on my reading list for quite some time, and I found it so stimulating that I read it from cover to cover on a six-hour flight to Seattle. The book describes the concepts of design thinking in a simple but enriching way, and the applications Brown draws to our daily lives had me unfolding idea after idea of how it could be applied to healthcare. At the time, I had already begun writing *The Patient Revolution*, but was so inspired by Brown that I scratched my initial drafts and constructed an entirely different approach.

I used the design thinking process as a framework for this book and to organize my thoughts. I also wanted to shed light on how the human-centered approach can be applied to the healthcare system, both broadly and to individual healthcare issues. Needless to say, this book is very much inspired by Brown's ideas. And while that may have been the best thing that happened to it, I did take a mini-vacation from my reading list to spare myself the possibility of starting over again.

What's Your Healthcare Experience?

In his book, Brown says that whether we're sitting on an airplane, shopping for groceries, or checking into a hotel, we aren't just carrying out a function, but having an *experience*. The same is true when we engage with the healthcare system, but despite our attempts to be patient-centric, we don't always consider the experiences of individuals as they move through the system. Moreover, our approach to health, arguably the most important aspect of our lives, still lacks personalized experiences that create opportunities for active participation.

Creating those experiences is, of course, not easy. Healthcare, unlike many other systems, isn't a single stream of predictable and regular events. It's uniquely personal to each individual, and that's what makes it so difficult to personalize. Like Dr. Marty Kohn, chief medical scientist at Sentrian, says, unlike *Jeopardy*, healthcare is not deterministic; there's often no one right answer since many patients have multiple comorbidities. Each individual undergoes a unique health journey; hence there's no one story that characterizes *the* healthcare experience.

Take a moment to think about some of your experiences with the healthcare system, perhaps a simple event, like your annual physical exam, or something more complex, such as a surgery that required extensive pre-op and post-op care. What series of events occurred throughout the process? Do you think that those activities catered to what's desirable to you? Did you find yourself actively participating or passively consuming?

The Experience Economy

Joseph Pine and James Gilmore say we're now living in what they call the "experience economy," in which people shift from *passive consumption* to *active participation*.[5] Services across most industries have fully shifted toward delivering experiences, and most have gone beyond that to provide personalized and customized experiences. This is what Pine calls the *transformation economy*, which is the final stage in his chain of economic value. In the transformation economy, services are designed so specifically for a person that they are life-transforming for the individual.[6] In other words, the experience changes us in some way.

If you're an online shopper like me, you're very aware of how the growth of the experience economy and the emergence of the transformation economy have revamped the online shopping experience. Not only is your shopping personalized to your likes and dislikes, but your experience is *your* unique experience. That means a retailer learns things about you like your lifestyle, preferences, and shopping habits, so that they can be proactive in giving you a truly personalized experience. And with new innovations like smart watches and one-click shopping, the mobile shopping experience is becoming an increasingly fun and engaging part of our lives. For example, products like the Google Ventures–backed Spring (www.shopspring.com) are attempting to re-create the shopping experience with a "one-click-to-buy" feature. And other industries, like financial services and hospitality, are making similar transformations; with services like Mint (www.mint.com), you can manage your financial health through personal budget and goal-setting, and receive custom recommendations for saving money. Even hotels are tailoring each part of the experience for guests, from entertainment and technology to pricing and communications.

These services are focusing on the *total* experience for their customers, which makes the experience continuous and all-inclusive. It's no longer about a one-night hotel stay or your one sporadic shopping spree; hotels and retailers are now customizing experiences for you before, during, and after your service. So now you may be checking into your room early on your mobile device, preordering television programs and snacks before you even arrive, and receiving personalized recommendations of places to eat near your hotel. And after you leave, you may receive promotions and offers catering to your preferences, encouraging you to plan another stay at the hotel. It's a continuous relationship that keeps you actively participating while blending into your daily rituals, like texting or perusing your Twitter feed.

Now think back to your healthcare experiences from earlier. Do they feel as seamless and continuous as these others? Do you feel like an active participator in your healthcare before, during, and after services?

Experiences are important to products, services, and systems because, simply put, they create happier customers. The key to excellent experiences is to focus on totality and consider every element across people, process, and place. By creating an unwavering consistency in delivering value, experiences result in more engaged and more satisfied customers. It's not an easy thing to do, but is entirely possible with the right understanding of your end-users and the right tools. I'll talk more about this later, but first, let's take note of what's going on today with the healthcare system.

#HEALTHCARETRENDS

The Affordable Care Act (ACA), also known as Obamacare, has since its inauguration in 2010 prompted a variety of transformations throughout the healthcare system. And while it's been a topic of ongoing debate since its inception, the ACA has brought forth many innovations toward a new health economy focused on consumer value. Healthcare payers, providers, and policymakers are exploring new initiatives to improve the health of individuals while managing the escalation of costs, including new service and payment models. Marketplaces are being created for consumers to purchase healthcare insurance, researchers are examining novel datasets to advance the field of precision medicine, and much, much more. Lots of unprecedented activity is taking place at all levels of the health ecosystem.

Volume to Value

If you're in the healthcare industry, you've likely heard by now of the paradigm shift that's happening from volume-based care to *value-based care*. The traditional "fee-for-service" model of healthcare reimbursement is well on its way out, as value-based payment is quickly becoming the new norm. This means that instead of being paid by the number of visits, procedures, or tests, providers are now being paid on the value of care they deliver to individuals. The switch has really turned the traditional model of healthcare reimbursement on its head, causing providers to change the way they bill for care. Providers are taking on more of the risk, as new payment models that reward outcomes and penalize poor performance, such as high rates of readmission and hospital-acquired conditions, are proliferating. These models require teamwork and collaboration between physicians, and many provider groups are establishing *accountable care organizations* (ACOs) to facilitate this. ACOs are teams of care that are accountable to the patients they serve and focus on the complete care delivery of patients and of populations. They require a high level of coordination among providers and the use of data and technology to succeed.

Insurance Marketplaces

The Health Insurance Marketplaces is one of the flagship components of the ACA, which is underpinned by the goal of improving access to healthcare across the nation. Each state was required to establish an insurance marketplace or participate in a federal exchange by January 1, 2014. By establishing marketplaces and mandating that insurers must sell coverage to all people with no price variation based on health status, the ACA has boosted the creation of retail-style health insurance. The exchanges encourage individuals to shop, compare pricing and coverage options, and select a health plan as an informed consumer. It's exciting to think that people who may have never had health coverage before now can at an affordable rate. The second year of open enrollment closed with about 11.7 million people signing up for coverage on the state and federal marketplaces.[7]

As health insurance moves from a business-to-business (B2B) model to a business-to-consumer (B2C) model, Pricewaterhouse-Coopers predicts that insurers will continue to zero in on the notion of consumer-directed health, as plans focus on the consumer experience across all lines of business and not just the individual market.[8]

Interoperability

Interoperability describes the extent to which systems and devices can exchange data and interpret that shared data. In 2009 came the big launch of interoperability efforts as healthcare reform began to push heavily for the digitization of health records through electronic medical records (EMRs)/electronic health records (EHRs), and patient portals. An incentive program called Meaningful Use was put in place by the federal government to encourage providers to meaningfully use EHRs. Meaningful Use sets specific objectives that providers must achieve to qualify for the incentives, and the objectives include things like improving quality, safety, and efficiency; reducing health disparities; engaging patients and families; improving care coordination; and maintaining privacy and security of patient health information.[9] Providers have certainly got on board, as Centers for Medicare and Medicaid Services had delivered payment incentives to more than 468,000 healthcare providers as of July 2015.[10]

The year 2009 also saw the State Health Information Exchange (HIE) Cooperative Agreement Program (State HIE Program), which offered states and territories $564 million in funding and guidance to enable secure electronic information exchange. According to the federal government, the purpose of the State HIE Program is to "facilitate and expand the secure, electronic movement and use of health information among organizations according to nationally recognized standards."[11] While each state now currently has some sort of exchange in place for the sharing of healthcare data, there's still significant progress to be made in interoperability. The ultimate goal is to create a national health information network, and that's why the Office of the National Coordinator of Health IT (ONC) released a ten-year roadmap for nationwide interoperability in January 2015. It's a wonderful vision to work toward and definitely puts forth the awareness that interoperability is a key priority over the next decade.

Other Trends

Aside from value-based care, insurance marketplaces, and interoperability, trends like transparency, focus on prevention and wellness, and reduction in fraud, waste, and abuse have all surfaced due to healthcare reform. Additionally, state governments have taken on a lead role in healthcare reform, through Medicaid expansions, by leading payment reform initiatives, and by creating new healthcare exchange models and databases like all-payer claims databases.

While many may argue that these changes are long overdue, it's still very inspiring, as it's setting the groundwork for creating better healthcare experiences and improvements to the delivery of care.

NOTES

1. "Relieving Pain in America: A Blueprint for Transforming Prevention, Care, Education, and Research." Institute of Medicine (IOM) report. http://iom.national academies.org/reports/2011/relieving-pain-in-america-a-blueprint-for-transforming-prevention-care-education-research.aspx.
2. http://consumer.healthday.com/bone-and-joint-information-4/backache-news-53/low-back-pain-leading-cause-of-disability-worldwide-study-686113.html.
3. U.S. Social Security Administration, Fact Sheet, February 7, 2013.
4. Tim Brown, *Change by Design*, 49. Harper Collins http://www.harpercollins.com/9780061766084/change-by-design.
5. https://hbr.org/1998/07/welcome-to-the-experience-economy.
6. http://www.strategichorizons.com/documents/BattenBriefings-03Fall-Frontiers OfEE.pdf.
7. U.S. Department of Health and Human Services, Office of the Assistant Secretary for Planning and Evaluation, "Health Insurance Marketplaces 2015 Open Enrollment Period: March Enrollment Report," March 10, 2015, http://aspe.hhs.gov/health/reports/2015/MarketPlaceEnrollment/Mar2015/ ib_2015mar_enrollment.pdf.
8. http://pwchealth.com/cgi-local/hregister.cgi/reg/pwc-hri-aca-five-year-anniversary.pdf.
9. http://www.healthit.gov/providers-professionals/meaningful-use-definition-objectives.
10. http://www.cms.gov/Regulations-and-Guidance/Legislation/EHRIncentive Programs/DataAndReports.html.
11. http://healthit.gov/sites/default/files/CaseStudySynthesisGranteeExperienceFinal_121014.pdf.

CHAPTER **2**

Insight

When we kicked off the design thinking process for Remedy by learning about others' pain experiences, we were coming across a wide variety of stories—from people with post-surgery pain and arthritis, to those with sciatica, back pains, and neck pains. I spoke with young adults in their late teens and early twenties with pain from playing sports and from technology overload, and middle-aged individuals who had undergone various surgeries and who were dealing with autoimmune conditions. Despite the depth and breadth of these experiences, I found common themes and patterns in the stories that made it very clear what the challenges of managing pain are, as well as what the desirable experiences are. Furthermore, these insights gave me a great deal of empathy for those who suffer with long-term chronic pain.

During this discovery stage, I found there was a strong consensus among pain patients about what things could be improved. Things like an easier way to track pain and share pain history, access to an expert when in pain, and more quality time with care providers, among many other things, were illuminated in my research. These insights were so enlightening because they validated my thinking and helped me to truly put people at the center of Remedy—the way we should approach every aspect of healthcare.

■ ■ ■

Our healthcare system is flawed and it epitomizes Tim Brown's statement that many of our large-scale systems fail to deliver a respectful, efficient, and participatory experience. Most of us can easily call to mind a healthcare experience that was less than ideal, whether you didn't find your doctor's appointment helpful, your visit involved a long wait time or was too costly, or some other combination of factors. And while the healthcare industry has talked the talk of being predictive, preventive, personalized, and participatory in healthcare (sometimes referred to as P4 medicine), we still lack the systemic execution to achieve these goals. And in defense of our industry, the requirements are not always as clear-cut as, say, the need for mobile hotel check-in. In part due to the diversity in the healthcare ecosystem, and challenges like the lack of standardization and inadequate digitization of health information, functional gaps between payers and providers, increase in regulations, and complexities with reimbursement, our ability to achieve a human-centered system has been hampered. We repeatedly hear about the larger quantifiable issues of today's system—the $3.5 trillion (and growing) healthcare bill, targets for reduction in hospital readmissions, the cost of expanding Medicaid, and the number of people without coverage. But it's not often that we hear stories about people who feel powerless in the system, who were diagnosed too late, who were denied care, or even of those on the other end of the spectrum, who've had multiple wonderful healthcare experiences. While quantifiable information is important, it doesn't get us to understanding the core of our issues. Nor does it tell us what we're doing well so that we can do more of those things even better. If we really want to achieve the goals of personalized healthcare, we need to systematically align our goals across the ecosystem to truly focus on the patient. We need to define patient-centric by hearing from patients themselves about what they desire, what motivates them, and how healthcare can be better integrated into their daily lives. It's time for the healthcare system to put humans at the center of the story so that we can focus on what healthcare should be about—keeping people healthy.

THE EXPERIENCE BLUEPRINT

I decided to go out on a journey to find meaning behind "patient-centric" from patients themselves, with the goal of sparking dialogues around what our typical and desired experiences really are. I started with discovery (Figure 2.1), conducting workshops and interviews and taking in all of the insights I could find regarding individual healthcare experiences.

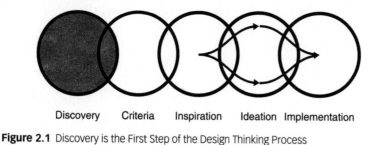

Discovery   Criteria   Inspiration   Ideation   Implementation

Figure 2.1 Discovery is the First Step of the Design Thinking Process

As I had done with pain patients, I wanted to learn about challenges and problem areas and see a variety of healthcare experiences through the eyes of the patient.

Doing this for an entire system is *much* different than for a focused issue. At the time, I wasn't even sure if this was a good idea because there are simply too many diverse experiences and challenges to possibly capture within the healthcare system. But, undaunted by the prospective information overload, I gave it a shot.

And I'm glad I did. As with the pain research, I was capturing a wealth of valuable information. And more important, I was gaining real insights, which, as Brown says, don't usually come from reams of quantitative data that measure exactly what we already have and tell us what we already know (think $3.5 million healthcare bill). The insights were, as expected, plentiful, and capturing them was only the first task; organizing the information was the second, and more challenging, hurdle. I ended up with a wall full of colorful sticky notes (truly, a piece of art), which helped me to find patterns, trends, and themes in the information.

The first thing I found by listening and compiling stories was that the majority of people fell into one of three buckets. There were those who interact with the healthcare system when they're healthy—the smallest group; those who interact with it when they get sick—a slightly bigger group; and the remainder (most people) who do when they're sick for a prolonged period. I called these groups the *proactives*, the *responsives*, and the *reactives*, respectively.

- *Proactives:* The proactives were by far the least common of the bunch, and are characterized as being very involved in their health and healthcare. Not only are they consistent with engaging in preventive care, such as primary care visits and various screenings, but they are determined self-care seekers. Many of them use technology and mobile health applications to track and monitor their health, and in general are very mindful about their health and wellness. They're self-motivated and their behaviors show this.

- *Responsives:* The responsives had a bigger presence than the proactives, but not as large as I had expected. This group is characterized by responding to the situation at hand. They engage with the healthcare system when they get sick, and if there isn't a trigger or red flag, then they continue on with relatively little motivation to improve their health.

- *Reactives:* Most people fit into this group. Like the responsives, these individuals require a trigger to engage with the healthcare system, the difference being that the reactives usually require multiple triggers, therefore engaging with the system when they're really sick or when their illness has progressed beyond onset. These individuals have little motivation and seem to have uncertainty toward doctors because of past experiences, money, insurance coverage, or other factors. This doesn't mean, however, that they aren't concerned about their health. It's simply not top of mind or as much of a priority as it may be for the proactives.

The illustration in Figure 2.2 shows the three groups and their unique engagement points with the healthcare system (noted by stars). When I put this into a visual form, one thing was very clear: Because so many people engage with the system when they're sick or really sick, there are a ton of missed opportunities to add value to patients *before* the onset of sickness. In other words, there are more opportunities to focus on *health*, not just care, and *wellness*, not just sickness. More on that later.

Despite the fact that proactives, responsives, and reactives differ in when they engage with the system, I found, across the three groups, that people typically had very similar challenges and sentiments when they do get sick and actually engage with the healthcare system. So after my sticky-note exercise, I found that the best way to depict a typical experience was to utilize a story that captured all of the themes I was finding to create an *experience blueprint*.

Experience blueprints are a human-centered design tool that's an enlightening and fun way to track how people travel through an experience in time. Its function is to illuminate unmet needs, identify the most meaningful points, and then turn them into opportunities. And more important, because they're based on observation, not

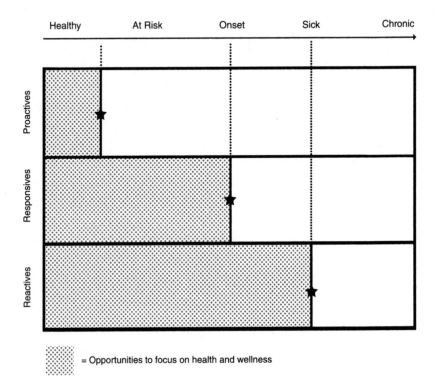

Figure 2.2 Engagement Points of Proactives, Responsives, and Reactives with the Healthcare System

assumption, they let us connect the user experience with the business opportunity.

For my blueprint, I decided to use my friend Dennis's story. Dennis's story resonated with me personally because a similar experience is what prompted me to create Remedy. Moreover, because it encapsulated most of the themes that I found across everyone's experiences, it was the perfect story to create a blueprint of (Figure 2.3).

DENNIS'S STORY

Take a moment to look through the blueprint. It may be helpful to use the blueprint as a guide while you read the story.

The experience begins with Dennis having pain in his pelvic area after a ski trip with his buddies. Dennis, being a typical reactive,

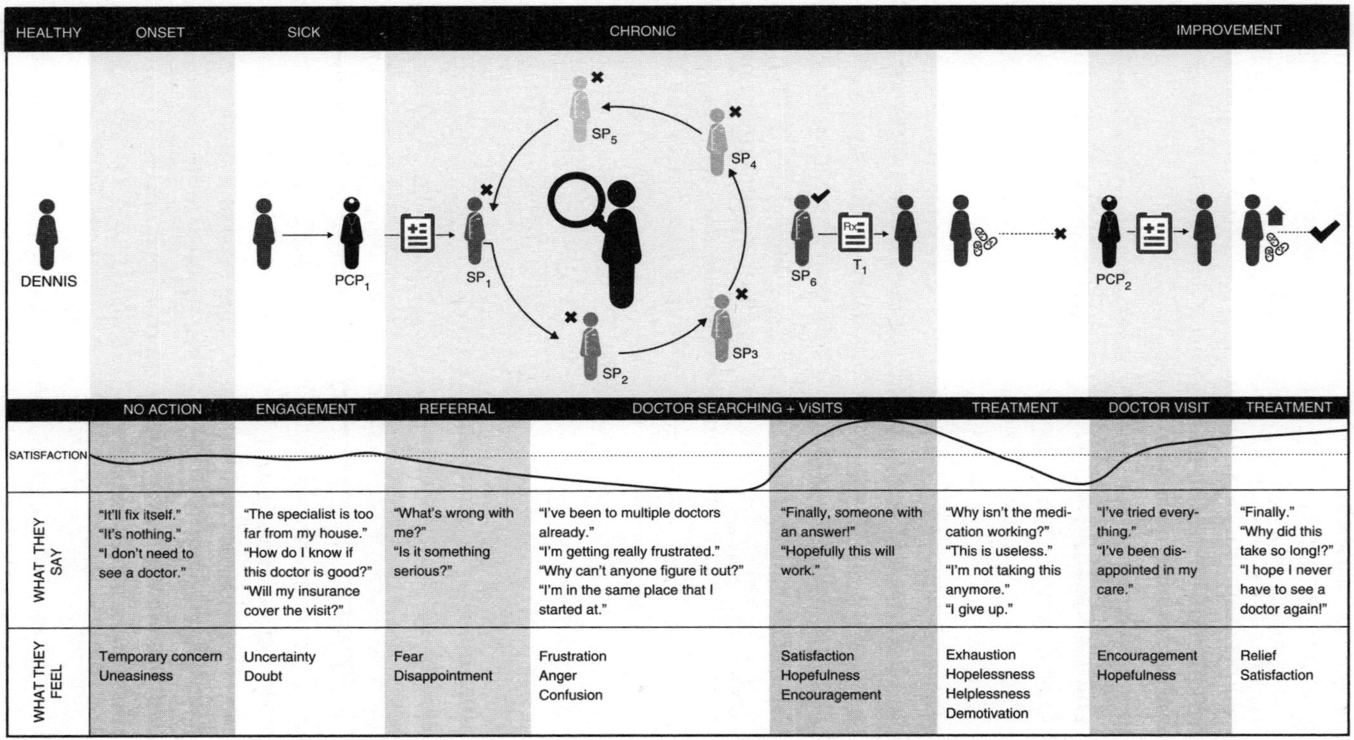
HEALTHY
ONSET
SICK
CHRONIC
IMPROVEMENT
DENNIS
PCP1
SP1
SP2
SP3
SP4
SP5
SP6
Rx
T1
PCP2
NO ACTION
ENGAGEMENT
REFERRAL
DOCTOR SEARCHING + VISITS
TREATMENT
DOCTOR VISIT
TREATMENT
SATISFACTION
WHAT THEY SAY
"It'll fix itself." "It's nothing." "I don't need to see a doctor."
"The specialist is too far from my house." "How do I know if this doctor is good?" "Will my insurance cover the visit?"
"What's wrong with me?" "Is it something serious?"
"I've been to multiple doctors already." "I'm getting really frustrated." "Why can't anyone figure it out?" "I'm in the same place that I started at."
"Finally, someone with an answer!" "Hopefully this will work."
"Why isn't the medication working?" "This is useless." "I'm not taking this anymore." "I give up."
"I've tried everything." "I've been disappointed in my care."
"Finally." "Why did this take so long!?" "I hope I never have to see a doctor again!"
WHAT THEY FEEL
Temporary concern Uneasiness
Uncertainty Doubt
Fear Disappointment
Frustration Anger Confusion
Satisfaction Hopefulness Encouragement
Exhaustion Hopelessness Helplessness Demotivation
Encouragement Hopefulness
Relief Satisfaction

Figure 2.3 Experience Blueprint of Dennis's Story

decides to wait it out before he jumps the gun on seeing a doctor. But, disappointed that the pain was only getting worse and was affecting many of his daily activities, Dennis decides to seek medical attention and visits his primary care physician (PCP). Following his appointment with his PCP, he goes through a whirlwind of referrals and sees many specialists, including proctologists and urologists.

Let's look at the first couple of steps and see what Dennis and others in this stage said and felt. When Dennis begins to feel discomfort, there's some feeling of apprehension and uncertainty about the illness, but it is overcome as Dennis thinks the issue will resolve with self-care or over time. A common statement made by individuals in this stage is "I don't think I need to see a doctor for this. It'll resolve itself." People ponder the idea of seeing a doctor, but wait it out to see if they feel better, just like Dennis did. They do this for a variety of reasons; either there's a strong lack of motivation or caring, they think there's a way they can resolve the issue on their own, or they don't want to pay for the doctor's visit because it isn't worth their time and money. In other words, they don't see value in it.

In the next stage, when the pain isn't getting better and Dennis goes to his PCP, he starts feeling uncertain when his physician provides him a referral. Many patients in this stage voiced that they want more information and more choices for referrals and to not feel limited in going to a certain specialist. They said things like, "The specialist is too far from my house," "How do I know if this doctor is good?," and "Will my insurance cover the visit?"

Next, Dennis goes to the recommended specialist and is disappointed by the lack of knowledge the doctor has about his issue. He subsequently does his own research, searching for recommended specialists who are covered under his insurance, and makes a couple of appointments over the next month. After virtually no success, not only does Dennis feel like he's wasting time and money, but his frustration is escalating. Further, he's not happy that he has to tell his story multiple times, which can be difficult when several events have occurred.

Dennis finally finds a urologist who believes he can help. Thinking that it's a bacterial infection, the doctor puts Dennis on an antibiotic.

Dennis is satisfied and encouraged by a potential treatment plan, but eventually a year passes and Dennis is still in pain. He loses motivation.

Many of us have experienced a similar situation in which diagnosing a condition takes longer than we'd like. These situations often lead to frustrated patients who believe that there's nothing more to be done about the issue, and they subsequently disengage completely from the healthcare system. This is an especially common scenario for chronic pain patients; many individuals feel after a certain point that there's nothing to be done about their pain, and that it'll just have to be a part of their life.

As Dennis's frustration rises, he begins to lose trust in his urologist, whom he was initially encouraged by. Many thoughts go through his mind, including, "Why isn't the medication working for me?" and "Do I even need this medication?" Dennis stopped taking it as his motivation plummeted. At this stage, there's a feeling of nervousness and apathy in addition to feeling ignored and out of control.

Dennis decides to give up. The mistrust in doctors, the waste of time and money, the inability to find a good doctor, and other factors all drive Dennis away from the healthcare system. As a result he lives with the pain while it continues to deter his day-to-day activities.

Flash forward two years to when Dennis has a job-mandated health check and is asked by the physician if there's anything else he wants to talk about. Dennis relates his story about the pelvic pain, and this time his physician is very confident about finding a remedy for Dennis.

Dennis was encouraged by the way the physician listened to his story and was able to correctly diagnose the problem as a torn ligament on the pelvic floor—a common sports injury. After that, the treatment that Dennis went through had him 90 percent better within the next five months. Finally, almost three years later, Dennis was pain-free!

DEFINING MY CRITERIA

Dennis's story may sound familiar to you. Most people who participated in sharing their stories, whether they were proactives, responsives, or reactives, faced many of the same challenges that Dennis did.

While lots of enlightening thoughts surfaced during the interviews, the following ones stuck out to me the most because they seemed to be recurring themes.

- ■ "Doctors should approach health more holistically and try to get a whole snapshot of patients' activities, lifestyle, and mental health."
- ■ "Long-term use of a medication without improvement should flag that the medication isn't working."
- ■ "Nothing wrong with a mistaken treatment, but at some point a doctor should change therapy or admit he or she doesn't know and refer patient to another doctor with more experience to make additional observations."
- ■ "A tracking system to let doctors know what other doctors are working on would be helpful. If a doctor can see other specialists are working on something, they may consult them to get a better understanding of a patient. I think currently they have an attitude of not stepping on toes and almost *never* talk to each other from separate practices."
- ■ "A tracking system for patients to keep abreast of medications, activity, and so on, to show the doctor long-term stats on following program."
- ■ "Patients should feel free and be encouraged to seek second, third, and fourth opinions if necessary if they feel they are not being treated medically correctly. Doctors should *ask* and get feedback from patients to see if they are satisfied with service and remedy."

Hearing these thoughts and patient stories, learning how people felt, and seeing the issues through their eyes made me think differently about our broader healthcare system. These stories illuminated seven key issues.

1. *Motivation:* Motivation appeared as a central theme across each stage of the experience. Whether it was the motivation to see a doctor, to adhere to a treatment plan, or to visit a specialist, maintaining a steady level of it seemed to be problematic for not

only Dennis, but for many of the interviewees. More broadly, people just weren't incentivized to make health a priority; things like healthy eating, annual checkups, and regular exercise schedules, people said, were things that "can always wait."

2. *Adherence:* This one's an offshoot of motivation, but an important one to note, as many individuals, including Dennis, voiced that sticking to doctor's orders is sometimes difficult. Whether it involves taking a pill, performing an exercise, recording their blood pressure daily, or going in for follow-up appointments, patients find it difficult to adhere across many stages of the experience, especially sticking to treatment plans.

3. *Choice:* Patients want the power of choice. They want to choose their own doctors, have a say in their treatments, know up front how much a visit or procedure will cost them, and be empowered to make their own choices regarding all aspects of their health.

4. *Coordination:* Much of patient frustration lies in the fact that our system lacks coordination. Patients find it difficult to relay their health stories to multiple disconnected individuals, and since many of us can't even remember what we ate for lunch yesterday, dictating a health story is frustrating.

5. *Effectiveness:* Patients want effective treatment, and it appears that in our volume-based system, physicians' focus on efficiency sometimes inhibits effectiveness. They want doctors to focus on quality of care, and for doctors to have enough time to effectively collaborate with them. The lack of time spent with providers was a big concern, and one individual went as far as to say, "We're like cattle being herded," referring to the way patients go in and out of the doctor's office. Individuals also said that more engagement and follow-up was necessary on how treatments are progressing between visits. In Dennis's case, he was taking an antibiotic for almost a year, only to find out that his condition wasn't bacterial in nature. He noted that monitoring how treatments are working, and if they're not working, is critical. People want feedback on that and time with

their provider to discuss these types of things. This is people complaining about the flaws of our volume-based system.

6. *Diagnosis:* This requires a category of its own for as many times as it came up. Misdiagnosing or delayed diagnosis makes patients feel like they can't trust doctors; one experience ruins it for them. Patients want to know they're being diagnosed correctly, the first time, every time. One individual even mentioned, "Every time I've gotten a second opinion about something, it seems to be different than the previous one." She continued, "You never know who to trust."

7. *Personalization:* More than ever, patients are expecting doctors to treat them holistically. That's not just knowing the patient's history and details, but it's also providing personalized advice and personalized treatments that are right for them. One individual stated, "I think that doctors say the same thing to most of their patients." People recognize that each individual's health is unique and should be treated in a personalized manner.

Since these issues were the most meaningful and prevalent ones that I collected, they became my *criteria* (Figure 2.4).

Defining criteria is the next part of the design thinking process, where we use the information we found in the discovery stage to identify the biggest customer issues. We then take these issues and turn them into opportunities, starting by reframing them as "How might we?" questions. We use the How-Might-We? format because it suggests that a solution is possible and because it offers the chance to answer the questions in a variety of ways.[1] This also sets us up for innovative thinking.

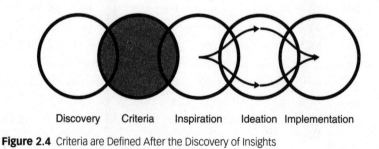

Discovery   Criteria   Inspiration   Ideation   Implementation

Figure 2.4 Criteria are Defined After the Discovery of Insights

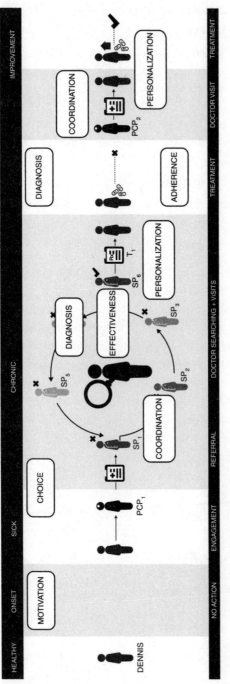

Figure 2.5 Criteria in Dennis's Experience Blueprint

Here's how I framed my criteria:

1. *How might we* encourage individuals to be more *motivated* in achieving better health?

2. *How might we* ensure patient *adherence* to treatment plans?

3. *How might we* create more opportunities for *choice* within the healthcare system?

4. *How might we* improve the *coordination* of care among healthcare providers?

5. *How might we* increase the *effectiveness* of healthcare services?

6. *How might we* increase the accuracy and timeliness of medical *diagnostics*?

7. *How might we* create more *personalization* of care?

In Figure 2.5, I've highlighted where each of the criteria appeared in Dennis's experience. As you can see, and as you probably recall from the story, some of criteria appeared multiple times, and some, like motivation and adherence, remained an issue throughout the entire experience. So it's important to think about the criteria across the entire spectrum of healthcare, not just at a specific touchpoint.

While the issues that surfaced weren't new to me, hearing them in context of personal experiences provided me with more insight into *why* they're pressing issues, and what changes patients would like to see in the healthcare system. If you're part of the healthcare industry, you already know that many of us have attempted to address these challenges, and in several cases have found success as well. But with patients voicing experiences like Dennis's, there's clearly still a lot of work to be done. Finding some inspiration is a good next step.

NOTE

1. http://www.designkit.org/methods/3.

CHAPTER **3**

Inspiration

L et's think back to the idea of Pine's transformation economy, in which experiences change us in some way. Healthcare, we know, is just beginning to extend into the experience economy, much less venture into the transformation economy, but it's the personalized, transformative experiences that are what's needed in healthcare. The industry may be just getting on board, but many others are much further along; in fact, they've thrived in both the experience and transformation economy. Banking, for example, is creating uniquely personal products and services that are transforming the way individuals approach their fiscal health. If banks can figure out how to motivate individuals to care about their fiscal health, surely there can be things done to motivate us to care about our physical health. What inspiration might be drawn from these other industries?

■ ■ ■

The design thinking process consists of three overlapping spaces: *inspiration, ideation,* and *implementation.* After conducting research in the discovery stage, and then identifying our criteria, the inspiration stage lets us think about the problems and opportunities we've found and search for solutions (Figure 3.1).

So naturally, I decided to look at other industries to find out how they've solved similar challenges—be it personalization, creating choice for consumers, increasing motivation, or improving coordination. I wanted to see what connections could be made to our healthcare system and what ideas could be translated to healthcare.

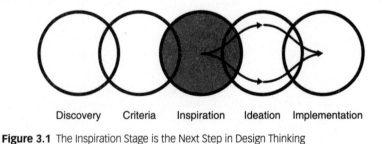

Discovery   Criteria   Inspiration   Ideation   Implementation

Figure 3.1 The Inspiration Stage is the Next Step in Design Thinking

LEARNING FROM BANKING

I mentioned the banking industry a couple of times now because it's one that's become increasingly personalized over the last decade. The banking and financial services industry looked a lot like healthcare 15 years ago. It was in general a reactive industry that certainly didn't focus on individual experiences and proactively assisting you to improve your fiscal health. But now, everything from personalized recommendations for savings to comprehensive views of your finances, to widespread mobile banking are all commonplace. Brett King, author of *Bank 2.0*, says, "The future of banking is about connections with your customers, engaging them when and where they need banking to solve a problem or provide a service. Banks won't be able to influence people with clever ad campaigns, better rates, or talk of branch networks. The only differentiation will be how you anticipate their needs and serve them in their day-to-day life, wherever they may be."[1] And this transformation is well on its way today.

Over half of U.S. adults with smartphones already use mobile banking,[2] and applications like Personal Capital and Mint, which provide customers the ability to manage their assets and investments and get advice on financial growth, are becoming the norm for managing finances. Banks are moving from segmenting and offering banner ads and mailers to offering a custom experience that leverages what the bank knows about that customer from across previous interactions and individual relationships. At the same time, however, while customers have embraced these new digital channels, they are also expecting higher value from face-to-face interactions at their bank branch. So the human factor is still very relevant, if not more important, and customers want to feel like their bank truly knows them, whether it's through a mobile or web experience or an in-person interaction.

A couple of scenarios from an Intuit report[3] helped me understand these concepts a little further. Let's look at Olivia's and Nathan's stories.

> Olivia is in her Realtor's office, checking her financial
> portfolio on her smartphone. She's considering purchasing
> a new home and wants to know how her bank can assist
> her. She opens a banking app to contact and work with

her personal banking specialist. A few minutes later, the specialist responds with an approved, customized financing package based on mortgage market data, an analysis of Olivia's income and expenses, and a risk-adjusted assessment of her banking history and investment portfolio. The bank also provides a property appraisal and suggests an opening offer. Olivia makes an offer based on her banker's input and closes the deal.

Nathan, chief executive officer of a manufacturing company, turns to a local bank for a financing package to help his firm expand. He worries that the bank will reject his application because his company, which focuses on product design and partners, has few tangible assets. As part of its risk assessment, the bank analyzed Nathan's social reputation and customer satisfaction, and included a sophisticated review of his intellectual property. Based on that, the bank concludes that Nathan is an excellent risk and offers terms better than he had expected.

Can you relate in some ways to Olivia and Nathan? You've likely experienced similar changes in your banking and financial services over the last few years; and if you haven't, get ready for it. These types of stories are becoming more and more prevalent as the industry ventures into the transformation economy, and will quickly become the norm.

LEARNING FROM RETAIL

The other industry that probably comes to mind when we think about personalized experiences is retail. We've all noticed customization while shopping, specifically online, for virtually any product—be it clothing, books, or household goods. Shoppers are becoming increasingly empowered and retailers are having to create unique experiences based on their preferences in order to succeed in the experience economy. I think this statement by Marti Tedesco, a digital marketer, sums it up pretty well:

The shopper drives the business now and retailers have to respond appropriately or the shopper will go elsewhere. Customers can easily bounce to another vendor—price and availability are 100 percent transparent on the web. This free movement leaves retailers with one primary way to differentiate themselves: through the customer experience.[4]

Retailers are using a plethora of techniques, both online and in stores, to create a pleasant and unique customer experience and establish loyalty among shoppers. Kohl's, for instance, recently tested real-time personalized offers in stores where shoppers can opt in for offers via their smartphones. If a shopper lingers in the shoe department, for example, they'll receive a coupon based on the shoes they looked at online but never bought.[5] The experience is therefore becoming seamless as the various channels are integrated. And what's more is that the in-store experience becomes much more valuable to the shoppers because of the integration of their online activity. This is similar to what I mentioned earlier regarding banking; customers, though they are utilizing multiple channels now, are expecting (and receiving) higher value from their experience in person. Digitization and tech haven't replaced the human element but, rather, have increased its significance.

Think about some of the promotions and offers you've received lately. Have you gotten any that have been spot-on for what you've been needing or wanting? I've been taken aback several times when I've received a suggestion or an offer from a retailer that I felt was an act of mindreading.

Many retailers, like Target, have switched from sending shoppers blanket email promotions to sending unique offers based on individual shopper purchases, going as far as to predict what you might buy on your next visit to the store. And like banking, mobile shopping is also becoming easier and more customized. Companies like Shop Spring and Trunk are creating new experiences for shoppers that include personalized fashion experts, one-click-to-buy features, and customized fashion feeds. There's no doubt that this industry is taking personalization and customer experience to a new level.

■ ■ ■

As I was reading back through these last few pages on the banking and retail industries, it was never clearer that what we need to create in healthcare are the very same things that these industries have established. Take a moment to glance back at the last couple of pages and notice some of the words that appear: *personalization, individual experiences, transparency, consumer connection, trust, loyalty, anticipating needs, engagement,* and others. Sounds a lot like what we're missing in healthcare, right? Both banking and retail have tackled many of the same challenges we experience in healthcare and that's why they're good sources for inspiration.

LEARNING FROM HEALTHCARE

But don't get me wrong. Although the healthcare industry is not as mature in today's experience economy, there are certainly sweeping changes happening in the industry that can serve as great sources for inspiration. For example, organizations like Privia Health—a physician practice management and population health technology company—are focusing on keeping people healthy, preventing disease, and improving care coordination in between office visits. They're creating a network of doctors dedicated to increasing people's engagement in their own health and well-being. Further, they're focusing on integrating health and wellness into people's daily lives. In other words, they're making healthcare more about the *total experience* that I talked about earlier, by creating patient-engagement before-and-after services, not just at the point-of-care. Similarly, Turntable Health, which describes itself as a "wellness ecosystem focused on everything that keeps you healthy," is changing the healthcare landscape completely. Its focus on team-based care, technology, and continuous service for its members is doing wonders for the patient experience. More important, the company is reinstating the human element of healthcare, building new models of care based on empathy and empowerment. It is empowering both doctors and patients—doctors to do what they became doctors to do, and patients to take more control of their health with the support and resources they need.

BUT HOW DO THEY DO IT?

You may be thinking, this all sounds great so far—banks, retailers, and healthcare organizations all creating better experiences for their clients, shoppers, and patients. The words sound nice, but how exactly are they making these bold changes?

The answer is simple. They're using data. More specifically, they're using big data analytics that generate new insights to make better decisions. They're using new types of data and new types of analysis to do novel things like predict, forecast, and optimize.

Let's start with some examples from the banking world. Over 70 percent of banking executives worldwide say customer-centricity is very important to them. They see it not only as key to understanding customer profitability, but also as the doorway to providing customers with a consistent and personalized experience.[6] Achieving customer centricity requires a deep understanding of customer needs and thoughts, and while demographics and current product ownership are at the core of customer insight, more insights are needed to get to this deep level of understanding. That's why behavioral and attitudinal insights are gaining importance in banking as channel selection and product use become more differentiated.[7]

Banks are moving from a traditional product focus to a unique customer focus through *customer experience management* (CEM), which is all about delivering personalized, contextual interactions that will assist customers with their daily financial needs. In addition, if done correctly, customer analytics in the context of CEM enables the real-time delivery of product or service offerings at the right time. By combining various data points such as past buying behavior, demographics, sentiment analysis from social media, along with CEM databases, banks are able to create specific micro—customer segments that help them to make more accurate decisions about their customers. These micro-segments capture new insights on customers that aren't obvious, for example, trends and patterns in the way customers respond to offers, and how factors like age and location affect buying behavior. Institutions can then use these segments for cross-selling and upselling, improving customer engagement, customer loyalty, and ultimately increasing sales and profitability while improving the customer experience.[8]

A great example of big data analytics in banking is the Royal Bank of Scotland (RBS), one of the largest banks in the world. RBS has developed an entire division dedicated to "personology," which Andrew McMullan, RBS director of analytics and decision making, says is all about using data to help the bank understand each of its customers. Using big data and analytics, the bank is re-creating personal relationships with customers that they believe disappeared some 40 years ago. Christian Neilissan, their head of data analytics, says of that time: "We knew our customers individually, we knew their families, we knew where they were in life, we knew what they were doing next."

In the 1980s, most banks lost focus on their customers and became more interested in creating products to meet sales targets. In the case of RBS, Neilissan said, "We had to get hundreds of thousands of credit card mailers out of the door. That was all that mattered.... The tactic may have boosted profits, but it left most customers with a feeling that RBS did not understand or care about their needs."[9]

That's why they're creating the personology team to analyze customer data and better meet their customers' needs. They've brought together multiple IT systems into a single data warehouse, and have invested in open-source big data technology, like Cloudera and Hadoop. The bank is using structured and unstructured data, and a variety of analytics methods, like decision trees, predictive analytics, and machine learning, to do things like identify customers who could save money by consolidating their loans, provide the best offers for each customer, and leverage mobile apps and online banking to spot patterns and tailor recommendations according to the customer's location and what they click on. Banks are also using data analytics to predict future behavior of customers, such as whether a customer is likely to make payments on time or the potential risk of losses or fraud.

■ ■ ■

Similarly, retailers are taking a parallel approach with data and analytics to enhance the shopping experience. They're combining product and customer data to get a *360-degree view* of their customers. Adding social media data to the mix to understand an individual's network, rather than just simply their own transactions, is helping to uncover trends and potential new opportunities with their customers. And even more, they're combining this with their customers' mobile activity to learn their behaviors. All of this allows retailers to send product recommendations and special offers directly to the customer's preferred device, taking into account all the information available.

Birchbox is one retailer that's really getting data analytics right. Birchbox is a beauty product subscription service that sends monthly boxes with different types of samples, with an opportunity to buy the ones that subscribers like. Online subscribers enter personal data like skin tone, hair color, and style preferences to determine what they receive each month, giving the company rich data to work with. This data also helps drive product recommendations in their brick-and-mortar store. In the store, customers have the ability to see samples up close before deciding to put them into their box. There are iPads throughout the store and a big touchscreen "Product Matchmaker" to make data-driven personalized recommendations.[10]

Birchbox also uses big data, like behavioral and survey data, when they launch a new service or offering, and to continuously improve their offerings. Deena Bahri, the VP of marketing, says that "from the beginning, data has been an essential part of Birchbox's growth and strategy...we use it to make important company decisions, and use it to guide us toward creating the best possible new products for our customers."[11] Birchbox is a highly personal brand all around, and being able to provide targeted products each month and suggestions in-store makes each shopper feel special. Plus, these micro-purchases can easily lead to loyalty that lasts a lifetime,[12] making it a win-win for Birchbox and its customers.

■ ■ ■

Both the retail and banking industries are great sources of inspiration in their data and analytics strategy. It's their use of these tools that's helping them and other industries to be successful in the experience and transformation economies. And while healthcare is beginning to make the shift to data-driven decision making, there lies ahead of us abundant, untapped opportunity to use data to impact the patient experience.

NOTES

1. http://thefinancialbrand.com/34839/ultimate-mobile-banking-experience-personalization/.
2. http://www.federalreserve.gov/econresdata/consumers-and-mobile-financial-services-report-201503.pdf.
3. http://http-download.intuit.com/http.intuit/CMO/intuit/futureofsmallbusiness/intuit_corp_banking.pdf.
4. http://www.retailtouchpoints.com/features/special-reports/retailers-seek-innovation-in-personalization.
5. http://www.forbes.com/sites/barbarathau/2014/01/24/why-the-smart-use-of-big-data-will-transform-the-retail-industry/.
6. http://fm.sap.com/data/UPLOAD/files/downloadassetBanks%20Betting%20Big%20on%20Big%20Data%20and%20Real-Time%20Customer%20Insight%20Bloomberg%202013-pdfbypassReg.pdf.
7. http://thefinancialbrand.com/46320/big-data-advanced-analytics-banking/.
8. http://thefinancialbrand.com/46320/big-data-advanced-analytics-banking/.
9. http://www.computerweekly.com/news/4500248239/Royal-Bank-of-Scotland-goes-back-to-1970s-values-with-big-data.
10. http://www.the-future-of-commerce.com/2015/02/27/big-datas-big-impact-personalized-shopping-experiences/.
11. http://mashable.com/2013/05/06/cmo-data/.
12. http://www.the-future-of-commerce.com/2015/02/27/big-datas-big-impact-personalized-shopping-experiences/.

CHAPTER **4**

Ideation

THE FUN PART

The ideation stage is the next step of the design thinking process (Figure 4.1), and it's also the fun part. In this stage we combine the understanding we have of the problem space and the people we're designing for with our imaginations to generate solution concepts. Ideation is about pushing for the widest possible range of ideas from which you can select, not simply finding a single best solution. So taking the inspiration we gained, the problems we found (our criteria), and what we learned about patient desires, what does the ideal healthcare system look like?

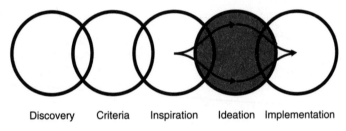

Discovery   Criteria   Inspiration   Ideation   Implementation

Figure 4.1 Ideation is the Next Step of Design Thinking

HEALTHCARE 2020

Last year, my friend and colleague Dr. Graham Hughes, who's chief medical officer at SAS, wrote a piece entitled "Healthcare 2020" that I think is appropriate to share in this chapter. Here are some of Graham's thoughts on a revolutionary healthcare system.

> It's August 1, 2020, and my heads-up display just sent me a priority health notification. I wasn't surprised, because I had used my newly downloaded phone app to walk me through the process of configuring my preferences for health notifications. When I opened the notification, my smart health app recommended five things I should do now if I want to reduce my chance of hospital admission by 20 percent next year, minimize my (ever increasing) out-of-pocket healthcare costs, and keep myself and my family as healthy as possible.
>
> I used to find these types of things irritating. Up to this point I'd wait until I met with my doctor at my annual

visit to be chastised with generic recommendations that didn't take account of my personal situation (like lose weight and try to reduce stress levels). Even worse, none of the advice was specific or actionable enough to follow or even remember. So, imagine how surprised I was when my doctor suggested that I try out this new app.

I'm told the app is based on a big data analytics platform. This doesn't mean much to me, except that it feels like it knows who I am and, very importantly, it gives me very specific recommendations and can even (wait for it) book recommended appointments, provide reminders, coaching, and encouragement, and has real time features that let me interact with real people who can help with anything I find confusing.

Another thing I like is that none of these recommendations are shared with anyone else yet—nobody at all. I like that, even though I plan on sharing some (but not all) of what it calls my "plan for health" with my doctor and other information with other members of my recently updated health team. Oh, yes, and it doesn't nag—unless I want it to.

So, I've used this app for a couple of months now, and it keeps on adapting. It links to my computers, my tablets, my phones, my heads-up display, and my TV. It keeps track of what I've done and where I am and pulls data automatically from selected social media accounts as well as a few of the health and fitness apps and devices that I use. What's even cooler is that no individual interaction or recommendation is the same as one I've had before, and I like that. It's definitely getting to know what motivates me and those things I'll need more help with, without me having to ask.

Last week, it recommended a time to Skype with my doctor to let her know how I was getting along with the app. I clicked OK and when the time came for our video call my doctor explained a little bit about how the app worked. Apparently what it does is use data from the setup process I completed when I installed the app to pull data from all the electronic health records held by the different doctors that I've seen in the past five years and from the hospitalization I had last year. It then pulls more information from my health insurance company and merges all that with the other data—such as home address, local air quality data, my credit card and other purchasing information, banking details, social media and health app accounts, as well as recommended medical literature and research from sites I preselected.

The app then compares me to hundreds of thousands of other people like me and combines that with additional information I provided relating to communication and escalation preferences, such as phone, email, video, or snail mail. What happens next I didn't fully follow, but it has something to do with predictive analytics and customer intelligence applications. Apparently other industries have been doing this for years, and it had become so transparent that I haven't even been aware of it for the past 10 years or so while shopping online.

My only comment to my doctor was: If the technology was available in 2014, why did I have to wait until 2020 to be able to use it for something as important as my health? For the first time ever, my doctor was speechless.

PATIENT EMPOWERMENT

Perhaps the most obvious characteristic of Graham's description of an improved healthcare system is that of patient empowerment: a shift of power to patients. To create better patient experiences and ultimately a better healthcare system, patients must be placed at the core of the system. And they, along with providers, must be empowered to make good decisions. The patient, as the consumer of healthcare, must be informed, invested in his health, and connected with healthcare resources he needs. And the provider must be incentivized to focus on providing the best care possible so that patients can be their healthiest.

With patients taking on more ownership of their health, a huge paradigm shift in responsibility is being made. Today, in most of our healthcare experiences, doctors are at the core of the system, serving as the primary authority figure and regulator (Figure 4.2). But in a new system, patients manage their health, their health network, and their health information (Figure 4.3).

This shift is what will revolutionize the role of the patient, by making him a *consumer* of healthcare. Just think—rather than the doctor

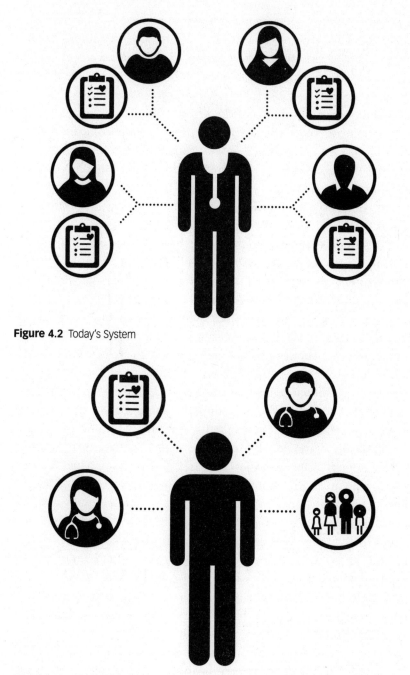

Figure 4.2 Today's System

Figure 4.3 New System

managing patients, the patients, or consumers, will manage their own health network. The consumer is the driving force within his "health team" of physicians and medical professionals, and has access to all of his personal health data, which follows him wherever he goes through all of his devices, be it a mobile phone or a wearable device.

Relationships are changed. The single relationship between doctor and patient doesn't exist anymore. Instead, relationships are more team-based, with continuous interactions occurring throughout the patient's health network. The relationship with the primary care provider is strong, and access to specialists isn't fragmented or difficult. Information is securely flowing to all of the necessary individuals and acts as the glue between teams of care.

Prevention is the norm, and we've moved from managing "sickness" to maintaining and improving "wellness." Connected by the data of the patient, all members of the health network are empowered with information that helps improve patient health.

Say goodbye to expensive sensors and devices. Our daily tech devices are our medical devices. And so are our nontech devices. Maybe our refrigerators are connected to our phones, which are connected to the lights in our office. We're provided with notifications and alerts for things like a prescription medicine that was left on the counter today, an alert that the irritation of the skin was caused by a new laundry detergent, or an alert for an abnormal heart rate that was sensed by a watch.

While there are already numerous tools out there, like Jawbone UP, Nike Plus, FitBit, and diet- and wellness-tracking apps, that are creating an immense amount of data on our health and lifestyle, most applications today aren't helping to measure progress and give feedback. In our new healthcare system, analytics works behind the scenes to deduce all of the rich information that is generated through multiple devices into digestible tidbits of insights that help us understand how our activities, habits, and behaviors promote or take away from our well-being. This provides us with a range of feedback, like early signs of disease and risk factors. More important, it provides us feedback on how we can improve our health each day.

Healthcare is less clinical and more personal, and it's become a part of our lifestyles. As consumers of healthcare, we're able to measure, assess, and be educated on our own health, as much or as little as we want. The new system encourages us to be preventive and proactive, and gives *personalized* a whole new meaning, as it becomes about the total experience rather than a single event. And my experience is completely unique to me; yours is to you. It even becomes fun. With rewards and incentives built across applications, we're encouraged to reach goals, self-diagnose, and consistently stay on track with a plan.

Our social network is connected to our health network, too. Our Facebook, Twitter, and Instagram accounts all feed into our repositories of data, adding an extra, crucial layer of information to our "personal health cloud." This addition provides insights on those things that affect our health that aren't directly part of our healthcare system—like how our relationships, the places we visit, the foods we eat, and even the people we interact with affect not only our physical but our mental health and well-being.

THE PERSONAL HEALTH CLOUD

The personal health cloud is where all of the magic happens. It's where all my health data is stored, analyzed, and shared from. It receives data that I generate, that my doctors generate, and others, like my insurance company, generate. But most important, the data I create makes my health cloud entirely different from yours. It gives me the freedom to include data that's relevant to my lifestyle and needs. My health cloud may include information such as my meals, my yoga schedule and the calories burned in each class, my sleep schedule, how many hours I sat on a plane, my travel schedule, and other things. It lets me pick what I want to include and ultimately looks at all of this information to find patterns and trends.

For example, the inputs of my health cloud may look something like Figure 4.4.

In a connected world, the health data cloud captures relevant information from all sorts of channels, which is what makes it so cool. Traditionally, data platforms only allowed decision makers to see a limited view of a person's healthcare, for example, just cost data from medical claims. But in the new system, we have the technology capability of collecting and assessing multiple views that can be shared with those we involve in our health—be it a doctor, a therapist, a dietician or other

Figure 4.4 Example of Inputs Into a Personal Health Cloud

medical specialist, our friends and family, or even our employers. And most important, the personal health cloud is used regularly by me—the patient, the consumer.

By pushing and pulling data to and from our everyday devices, it integrates seamlessly into our lives, so much so that we don't even know that it exists. Contrary to most of today's tools, it *guides* our behavior rather than just tracking it, and provides nudges, reminders, and suggestions to help us change our unhealthy behaviors.

But there's more to it than my cloud and your cloud. It's part of a larger platform, a larger health cloud. The larger health clouds capture information from personal health clouds to help our entire healthcare system (Figure 4.5). Individuals decide whether they want to contribute to a big data health cloud, and do it anonymously, so that people don't actually know who they are. By gathering information from billions of individuals, everyone from researchers to clinicians to patients benefits.

Because of new types of information—specifically, self-generated data—in the cloud, we find patterns and associations that help us learn about healthcare in new ways. It brings us to really insightful learnings about nonclinical factors that affect our health. And since 80 percent of health is impacted by factors *outside* of the healthcare system,[1] these findings create a novel, modern approach to healthcare.

Clinicians use the health cloud on a regular basis. It's easy to find similar patients to theirs to identify the best treatment plans. And by

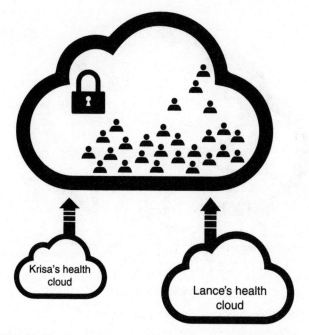

Figure 4.5 Health Cloud Receiving Information from Personal Health Clouds

similar, it's not just, for instance, two females who are 34 years old, of Asian descent, and weigh 130 pounds; it's also these two people with similar lifestyles, behaviors, and patterns. The health cloud automatically mines all of this data and reduces it to consumable insights really fast—and spits out information that clinicians can use for treating patients. And sometimes clinicians don't have to search for anything at all; this information is automatically generated and delivered on their patient's profile or health record. In other words, it lets clinicians interact effortlessly and gives them exactly the information they need at exactly the right time.

Patients also use their health clouds regularly. Besides getting personalized notifications, alerts, and reminders consistently, they also can share their personal health clouds with each other, create their own health clouds with their families, and receive helpful insights based on their family history (Figure 4.6).

It empowers patients to be an active partner in their health, and to have better, more meaningful interactions with their providers,

Figure 4.6 Personal Health Clouds can be Created for a Family

families, employers, and others involved in their health. The result is everyone is more informed and more engaged, and patients are more active participators in their own health than ever before.

NOTE

1. http://www.rwjf.org/en/library/features/health-policy/public-health-and-prevention.html.

PART II

Do

CHAPTER 5

Implementation
Part 1

Now that we've covered discovery, criteria, inspiration, and ideation, we can move on to the final stage of the design thinking process: implementation (Figure 5.1). In this chapter and in Chapters 6 and 7, I'll talk about how we can implement change and create an improved healthcare system. In part 1, I'll talk about the tools and technologies that are available to us in the healthcare industry, and in parts 2 and 3, I'll discuss how we can apply these tools to our criteria that we defined in Chapter 2.

FROM IDEAS TO REALITY

The implementation stage is about identifying how to implement game-changing solutions into people's lives. How do we take the ideas we created and make them a reality? It involves rapid prototyping, iterating, and testing of new ideas until we find something that works. While we can't actually prototype and test solutions within a book, we can use the principles of design thinking to identify and discuss solutions.

Design thinking uses the three lenses of *desirability, feasibility,* and *viability,* as shown in Figure 5.2, to find the best path to innovation. We already learned about what's desirable by gaining insights from individuals and laying out a vision for the ideal. But what is *feasible* from a technology perspective? And what is *viable* from a business perspective? In other words, what tools and technology are available to make bold changes, and what's a business strategy that will align with healthcare stakeholders—like payers, providers, and, of course, consumers. I'll talk first about tools and tech in this chapter, as they're key. The right tools are important because in order to innovate quickly, we

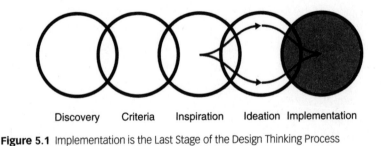

Discovery   Criteria   Inspiration   Ideation   Implementation

Figure 5.1 Implementation is the Last Stage of the Design Thinking Process

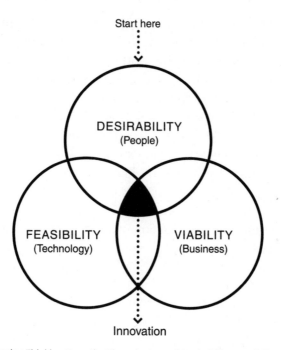

Start here

DESIRABILITY
(People)

FEASIBILITY
(Technology)

VIABILITY
(Business)

Innovation

Figure 5.2 Design Thinking Uses the Three Lenses of Desirability, Feasibility, and Viability

need to be able to test new things and also quickly change course if something's not working or needs to be modified.

TECHNOLOGY FEASIBILITY

The demands of a modern healthcare system require that we implement user-friendly solutions quickly that can make significant improvements to both the consumer and provider experience. Lucky for us, the same technologies that are used across industries like banking and retail are available to healthcare, and have already started to be utilized. Not only that, but these technologies are becoming cheaper, better, and faster, which makes creating new products and services with them a great opportunity for healthcare.

While traditional IT systems were massive and costly investments that moved slowly and allowed minimum functionality, modern IT systems are fast and efficient, and can handle massive amounts of information. For example, Hadoop is an open source software framework for running applications on large clusters of commodity hardware. It's a remarkably low-cost and scalable alternative to data servers of the past. Hadoop simplifies processes, operates at a much lower cost, and can support an ever-growing amount of information. Perhaps the greatest advantage of new-generation IT platforms like Hadoop is that they can harness all the disparate information across the ecosystem—whether it's clinical information through electronic health records (EHRs), laboratory results, healthcare claims, self-generated mobile health data, social media data, or any other type of information. Combining these big data technologies with *cloud analytics* can take this large amount of disparate information and turn it into valuable insights.

■ ■ ■

Cloud-based technology, is an agile, cost-friendly way to implement analytics that doesn't require installing and supporting multiple onsite technologies. That means it can be up and running quickly, and everyone in an organization can have easy access to powerful analytics through their Web browser.

Together, big data platforms and cloud analytics have redefined the possibilities for using data—terabytes and petabytes of it—to dramatically improve healthcare costs, the care experience, and patient outcomes. With these new tools, all of the elements of data analysis—data sources, data models, application processing, computing power, analytic models, and sharing or storage of results—can exist on a shared infrastructure. That means everything can be done in one space. Computing resources are virtualized and available on-demand on any device, and users get fast access to the answers they need from anywhere. These massively scalable platforms can store any amount or type of data, turn this data into valuable information, and provide it to users in a simple way. And it's exactly how health clouds can be established to improve the healthcare system.

It all starts with the data. Using data, healthcare, too, can adopt many of the same approaches to the experience economy as other industries have, defining the new role of the consumer of healthcare, creating better coordination among the entire system, driving personalized care and an overall more seamless and integrated experience for consumers. Data is most certainly the biggest and most critical tool in our toolbox.

BIG DATA

By now, we've all heard of big data. In today's digital world, big data is a part of every industry, and it's going to continue to grow rapidly as digitization and connectivity increase. In healthcare, big data is being generated at all corners of the ecosystem, and consumers, providers, and payers are all fueling this revolution. A number of data sources are driving this growth, including administrative data such as health-care claims data, clinical data such as EHRs, self-generated data such as that produced by fitness and wellness mobile applications and wearable devices, and patient-reported data such as surveys. Let's take a look at some of these data sources.

Medical Claims Data

Healthcare claims data is the most accessible, and structured type of health data in the United States, and it offers the broadest view of how healthcare services were delivered. It includes many elements that are valuable in understanding healthcare delivery. For example, aside from the amounts billed and paid, elements of a claim that are particularly useful are diagnosis codes (ICD-9 or ICD-10), procedure codes (CPT), the site of service, the date of the service, the length of an inpatient stay, the referring physician, and demographic information on the patient and provider. Claims data include many other components as well.

Claims are big data simply because of their nature—there's a claim for just about every health system transaction. Naturally, claims data is growing with the increase in population, and more recently, with the increase of insured individuals due to the health insurance marketplaces. With more access, more claims are generated, and many big data initiatives to gather this data have been under way. Because claims data adheres to national standards for format and with HIPAA transaction formats, integrating and analyzing across various claims databases is less complex than with other types of health data. It's also what makes it a good starting point for analyzing health data.

While claims data has traditionally acted as transactional data to support billing and eligibility, the new health economy has changed this. For instance, state Medicaid programs operate Medicaid management information systems (MMIS) that in the past simply collected claims data for business processes and billing; but now, programs are seeking to put this data into a cloud environment with a layer of analytics. With new enabling technologies that allow a single platform for big data and analytics, claims data is now an opportune source for analysis.

Clinical Data

Clinical data from electronic medical records (EMRs) or electronic health records (EHRs) has more depth of information than claims data, and it, too, is growing exponentially as health records continue to become digitized. Clinical data includes things like lab results, doctors' notes, vital signs, and more. With the increased adoption of EMR/EHRs, and the creation of *health information exchanges* to share clinical data among providers, clinical data is a growing and valuable data source for healthcare stakeholders.

Unlike claims data, one of the prominent challenges with clinical data is the saturation of clinical data systems across the healthcare continuum. There exists hundreds of various electronic health record systems, each with its own approach to clinical data management. Further complicating matters is the lack of a true data standard across the industry to assist in cross-system data integration efforts.

Self-Generated Data

Self-generated or self-reported data is data that's created either actively or passively through mobile or wearable devices, or other types of sensors. In healthcare, it's typically referred to as *patient-generated health data* (PGHD), but you don't have to be a patient to generate health data, so I like to refer to it as self-generated instead. It's all of the data people create while simply living their lives. Individuals today are monitoring and logging everything from calories burned to medications and supplements taken. Thousands of applications exist, and many more are being developed, to collect personal health and lifestyle data. Mobile health continues to grow exponentially and is expected to reach $20.7 billion by 2018, with nearly 96 million users.[1] People are either actively entering data about themselves, such as their daily food intake, or devices are passively picking up data on individuals, such as their heart rate or the number of steps walked. Not only is this the most exciting data source because it captures so many details unique to an individual, but it's also the biggest opportunity for innovation in health care. With over 100,000 mobile health and wellness apps, and the rise in consumer adoption of wearable technology—like smart watches, digital health trackers, and sensor-laden clothing such as smart running shoes—people are collecting and tracking an unfathomable amount of data on themselves. Further, with the connectivity that the Internet of Things (IoT) is bringing and will continue to bring, we'll see more connected homes, cars, and desks, and other things that will generate massive amounts of personal data.

Patient Satisfaction and Patient-Reported Outcomes Data

Patient satisfaction data is usually captured through surveys and measures how happy the patient was with his or her healthcare services. CMS, along with the Agency for Healthcare Research and Quality (AHRQ), developed the HCAHPS (Hospital Consumer Assessment of Healthcare Providers and Systems) Survey, also known as Hospital CAHPS, to measure patients' perspectives on hospital care. Not all hospitals in the United States participate, and some hospitals create their own surveys.

Patient-reported outcomes are data that patients provide on their health status for physical, mental, and social well-being. The National Institutes of Health (NIH) created a system called PROMIS—the Patient-Reported Outcomes Measurement Information System—to measure what patients are able to do and how they feel. This data helps provide clinicians and researchers with important patient-reported information about the effect of therapy that isn't available in traditional clinical measures. Patient-reported outcomes help clinicians to better understand how various treatments might affect what patients are able to do and the symptoms they experience.[2]

With the demand for improving the total healthcare experience, an emphasis on collecting patient satisfaction and outcome data has certainly grown. However, we can and should do better, and more efforts to collect this type of data must be initiated. I think Dale Sanders of Health Catalyst says it really well:

> My Toyota maintenance guy sends me a customer satisfaction email automatically after each "clinical encounter" with my cars. He asks me to rate the quality of the service he provided as well as the quality of the outcome ("Did we fix your problem?") and the cost effectiveness ("Do you feel that our prices were fair, clearly explained beforehand, and understandable?"). Toyota corporate offices review these results in detail and they hold those dealerships totally accountable, with consequences for bad numbers. You would think that the functionality of EMRs that costs millions of dollars could at least match my Toyota maintenance guy.... As a businessperson and a CIO, the only two metrics that really matter to me are employee satisfaction and customer satisfaction. As fellow CIOs can attest, we are inundated with metrics.... But the only two metrics that really matter are employee satisfaction and customer satisfaction. Every other metric is a means to those two ends.[3]

Getting feedback on what patients think of services and treatments is a critical layer of data that can help us in creating positive experiences within the healthcare system. Further, real-time feedback is always more valuable, and with the rise of digital technologies, we now have opportunities to capture that in new, accessible ways.

Social Media Data

Social media data, from sources like Facebook, Twitter, LinkedIn, or other channels, is a form of self-reported data. When we're doing things like checking into places, tagging people, and posting articles we like, we're generating data on the Web. Data elements such as sociodemographics, interests, likes, activities, and location can provide a wealth of insights on the nonhealth factors that impact health, which, as we discussed, make up more than 80 percent of total factors. Social media data is ever-growing, and things like trends, hashtags, key text, and locations of individuals can all help us to understand both individuals and populations.

Any Other Type of Data

Since so much of health is impacted by outside factors, and because the big data revolution is generating so much new information, healthcare systems can also consider utilizing nonhealth data to improve care. For example, education data and consumer research data can provide an even more detailed view of individuals and populations.

Data is not only our most valuable tool, but it's a requirement for succeeding in the experience and transformation economies. By the year 2020, healthcare data will be doubling every 72 days, says Stephen Gold of IBM. About a tenth of this data will involve treatment, another third will consist of genomic sequences for individuals, and half of that data will come from medical instruments and wearable devices.

"It is humanly impossible to keep up with this data," says Gold. "It is the Internet-of-Things on steroids." Gold is right, and keeping up with the data and benefitting from it will require big data analytics.

ANALYTICS

Data alone won't get us very far in establishing the health clouds of tomorrow and improving the healthcare experience. We need analytics to get value from all of this data.

At SAS, we define big data analytics as *the process of examining big data to uncover hidden patterns, unknown correlations, and other useful information that can be used to make better decisions.* That means processing and analyzing billions of rows of data, with hundreds of millions of data combinations, in multiple data stores and abundant formats. In other words, making sense of the massive amount of big data that's being generated.

Analytics is divided into three categories (Figure 5.3), and it's helpful to know something about each one.

Figure 5.3 Three Categories of Data Analytics

Descriptive

Descriptive analytics answers the questions about *what happened and why it happened*. It's sometimes referred to as reactive analytics because it gives us information on the past, like how many people enrolled, what the total costs were, and what age groups had the most ER visits last year. Descriptive analytics is also what you may know of as *business intelligence* (BI).

Predictive

Predictive analytics, on the contrary, lets us determine the probability of *what will happen next*. It's the use of data, statistical algorithms, and machine learning techniques to identify the likelihood of future outcomes based on historical data. Essentially, it's using data on the past to predict what may happen in the future.

A common type of predictive analysis is forecasting, which lets us determine the direction of future trends (think weather forecasts). In healthcare, forecasting can let us answer questions like: What are healthcare costs forecasted to be next year? How much will the cost of diabetes increase in five years? How many people will be eligible for health insurance coverage in 2017?

Prescriptive

Going a step further, prescriptive analytics tells us *what we should do next*; what's the optimal decision based on the predicted future scenarios? It gives us the outcomes of different choices and recommends the best choice.

Optimization, a prescriptive analytics tool, lets us identify the scenarios that will produce the best outcomes. Optimization is usually thought of as operational in nature; for example, you may have heard of optimizing workflow and resources. But it's more than that. Optimization can also tell us things like what the optimal health interventions are for an individual—things like identifying the likelihood of a patient responding positively to a treatment, and learning what the best combination of services if for an individual can be accomplished with optimization tools.

Text Analytics

Because 80 percent of today's data is unstructured, meaning it doesn't have a defined format (think tweets, likes, photos, video clips), we need text-mining tools to improve our predictive and prescriptive analytics. Text mining lets us capture important text from emails, notes, photos, comment fields, notes, and so on, and add it to our analytic models. For instance, capturing relevant text from doctors' notes within an EHR can help us determine if multiple physicians are finding a trend across an individual's visits or across a certain group of people. Using that information in our predictive models, we would be better able to predict everything from symptoms to ER visits.

Predictive, prescriptive, and text analytics are typically thought of as advanced analytics. They're more complex to create than descriptive analytics, and provide deeper levels of insight that help guide our decision making.

TRENDS IMPACTING ADVANCED ANALYTICS

Predictive and prescriptive analytics have been getting a big boost with recent technology trends like machine learning and the Internet of Things. These trends are important to know about as well as we continue our discussion on analytics.

Machine Learning

Machine learning is a method of data analysis that automates analytical model building. Using algorithms that iteratively learn from data, machine learning allows computers to find hidden insights without being explicitly programmed where to look. That means that the models get better the more we use them because they *learn*.

Machine learning isn't a new concept; it's been around for a while. But with the growing volume and variety of data, computing processing that is cheaper and more powerful, and affordable data storage, like Hadoop, machine learning is getting fresh momentum.

All of these things mean it's possible to quickly and automatically produce models that can analyze bigger, more complex data and deliver faster, more accurate results, even on a very large scale. And that means that our predictive analytics can become stronger and more accurate, without human intervention. It's called automated model building, where predictive models are built on their own. Think about Netflix or Amazon, for example. The more you use them, the more it learns about you, and everyone else who uses the service. Now imagine what it could do on an even larger scale, like genomics research or medical diagnostics. It's really exciting for healthcare because it's going to make diagnosing conditions faster, more accurate, and more accessible to providers.

Internet of Things

The Internet of Things is another tech trend that's taken off recently and that's really trailblazing for healthcare. Soon, our cars, our homes, our major appliances, and even our city streets will be connected to the Internet, creating this network of objects that's called the Internet of Things (IoT). It's a growing network of everyday objects—from industrial machines to consumer goods—that can share information and complete tasks while you're busy with other activities, like working, sleeping, or exercising. It's estimated that 30 billion objects will be connected by 2020.[4] Yes, you read that right: 30 billion! Can you imagine the enormous amount of data that'll be created from all of these 30 billion things? Everything from our refrigerators to our clothing could be connected, creating an unimaginable amount of information. From a healthcare perspective, this is a game changer for remote patient monitoring and self-care. Think about the insights that your physician could get from all of these connected things, from connecting your bed at home, for example, to your physician's digital devices to allow them to monitor you after a surgery, or for something even more astounding, like sending alerts to physicians about impending events, like a heart attack.

The opportunities for IoT are truly incredible, but it's important to note that the value is not in connecting things. It's in using all of the connected data to find patterns and trends, and using things like machine learning to automatically predict and prescribe. That's why Jim Davis, SAS's chief marketing officer, often says it's really the "analytics of things" that we should be talking about.

In an environment like the massive Internet of Things, It's mind-boggling to think about how to approach analytics. I think Jim breaks it down really well in one of his blog posts[5] with some key questions and answers:

> Q. With all the data out there, how can I store it efficiently?
>
> A. Hadoop.

I've talked briefly about Hadoop, and I'll explain it more in the next chapter, but Jim says we need to use Hadoop to create an analytics platform. Basically, you don't want just another place for data to sit. You want to run analytics inside the Hadoop environment; you want to do something with the data.

> Q. What if I need the data right away? How can I get it quicker?
>
> A. Streaming data.

I know I'm biased because I work for an analytics company, but streaming data is the coolest thing in the world. It's exactly what it sounds like: a continuous stream of data. Remember the heart attack example I gave earlier? Those types of situations, and most others related to healthcare, require us to act fast. The only way to catch something like that ahead of time is to have access to real-time analytics, meaning we need to analyze the data continuously as it comes in. Slow response times lead to lost opportunities, and that defeats the purpose of connecting all of our things in the first place.

Data streaming tools can process millions of events per second while finding and assessing issues. That way, red flags come up instantly and you're in a better position to prevent a negative situation.

Q. Now that I have access to all this data, where do I start?

A. Data visualization.

Visual analytics is a wonderful tool that gives you a way to easily explore and understand all of your big data. Instead of being bombarded with an overwhelmingly massive amount of numbers, visual analytics takes your data and turns it into pictures. And who doesn't like pictures? I'll talk more about data visualization in the next chapter as well.

Q. How can I use this data to discover new possibilities?

A. Advanced analytics.

This one's kind of a no-brainer. To get real value from the IoT, we need to move beyond basic analytics to the advanced analytics that we've been discussing—things like optimization, forecasting, text analytics, data streaming, and more.

Building an Analytics Strategy

Now that you know a little more about analytics, machine learning, and the Internet of Things, you've probably concluded that our opportunities for them in healthcare are infinite. And if you're like me, then you're probably questioning why we don't use them more in healthcare. The use of analytics in healthcare is in fact significantly behind other industries. That's one of the most prominent reasons why healthcare is lagging in today's experience economy. Although many healthcare providers and payers have begun to explore analytics, the industry as a whole has merely scratched the surface. In fact, only 10 percent of healthcare organizations use advanced analytics tools to capitalize on information, according to a 2015 survey[6] from KPMG. There's still a lot of greenfield to cover in the health analytics space.

Before we jump to analytics, though, we have to have a data management and data analytics strategy. I like to think about the strategy in terms of what problems we want to solve. That's where our experience blueprint and our criteria come back into the picture. Take a look back at the challenges we identified. Then, using what we know about our data sources, we can begin to think about how to use them to address these issues and identify what technology to use.

Privacy and Security

Even before all that, we need to think about critical issues such as privacy and security. Issues such as privacy and security aren't trivial, and any data analytics strategy must include policies for keeping patient identifiable data within the confines of permissible stakeholders, and for seeking permission of individuals for utilizing their data.

More broadly, as self-generated data proliferates, the U.S. healthcare system must create standards and policies for the sharing of these new types of data. Patients should have ownership of their personal health data, and the ability to choose whom, and at what level, to share their data with. Even further, as the Internet of Things expands, security must be tackled before smart digital devices begin transmitting and sharing data.

The Analytics Framework

After identifying how to handle privacy and security, we can start building our data analytics infrastructure that will establish our health cloud. The data infrastructure should identify what types of data we want to bring together, how to transform the data into usable formats, how to analyze it, and how to see and deliver the outputs to individuals. The data must be brought together in a meaningful way, be linked to connect the various data for each patient, and establish a 360-degree, or holistic, view of patients and of populations. It requires data integration and data quality processes, along with big data platforms like Hadoop. At SAS we're combining all of these technologies into a health analytics framework to make it simpler to create a single platform for analytics.

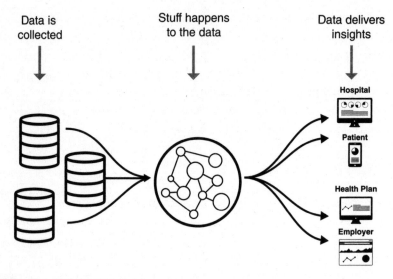

Figure 5.4 Analytics Framework

I like to think of the framework like Figure 5.4.

SAS's Mark Torr, director of the EMEA and AP Analytical Platform Center of Excellence, calls this approach a "big data innovation lab" in which Hadoop, commodity hardware, and cloud analytics provide a collaborative place for experimentation to take place around an organization. You can read more about the big data innovation lab in Mark's SAS blog.[7]

A Big Data Innovation Lab

As you can imagine, the sheer amount of data a healthcare organization can and does collect is staggering. Bringing all of this data together can be overwhelming; how do we know which data is relevant and usable? And do we need all of it? It was hard enough bringing together data when it was structured, but in the new age of big data, where unstructured data—such as hashtags, likes, and photos—is pervasive, how do we separate the valuable data from the irrelevant data? Do we risk losing valuable information if we leave out certain data elements?

This debate occurs across all organizations and industries when creating a big data analytics strategy, and these massive databases are often referred to as "data lakes." The Wiktionary definition for a data lake[8] is a massive, easily accessible data repository built on (relatively) inexpensive computer hardware for storing big data. Unlike data marts, which only store some attributes of the data, a data lake is designed to retain all attributes, especially for when you don't yet know what the scope of data or its use will be.

According to Mark, if you develop that idea further, the aim of deploying a data lake, based on Hadoop, is to move the majority of an organization's data into Hadoop, with a long-term goal of Hadoop becoming the predominant and only data store over time. This removes the need for the previous generation's enterprise data warehouse (EDW) and data marts.

However, since this isn't entirely possible for most organizations today, because of legacy systems like healthcare claims warehouses and existing EDWs, Mark says that the data lake is being redefined to represent the complete new data ecosystem an organization wants to build. That means Hadoop can be used without throwing out old databases. In other words, it can complement other databases and work in parallel with them to create a big data analytics strategy. Mark identifies three ways to implement this strategy, as shown in Figures 5.5 through 5.7. (*Note:* The cute little elephant represents Hadoop.)

1. Hadoop as a new data store (Figure 5.5).

    In this scenario, Hadoop will simply handle new types of data that are not yet currently stored in an EDW. For example, social media data and patient/self-generated data could be gathered with Hadoop, and claims and clinical databases could exist as they currently are. This strategy is practical if an organization wants to use Hadoop simply to support innovative business strategies that require new data, or as a way to get existing unstructured and semi-structured data into one location at the lowest cost. It doesn't affect existing databases, and is an option if an organization wants to use data that they've never used before.

2. Hadoop data platform as an additional input to the enterprise data warehouse (Figure 5.6)

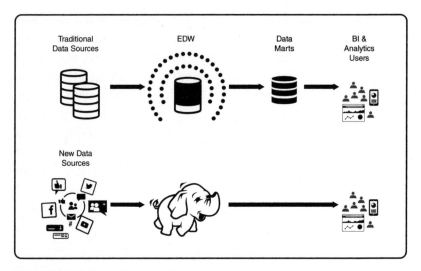

Figure 5.5 Hadoop as a New Data Store

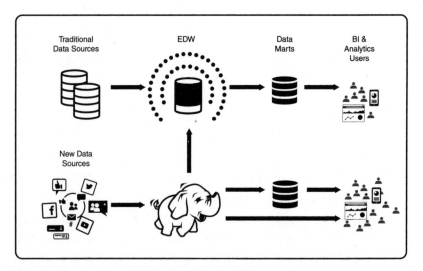

Figure 5.6 Hadoop as an Additional Input to the EDW

In this second option, Hadoop essentially complements the rest of the data strategy. Organizations can use Hadoop to handle new types of data, as in the previous scenario, but also feed the newly discovered insights into the EDW for mass consumption. The existing EDW process isn't impacted, but if something valuable is discovered in Hadoop, it can be added to the EDW. The idea here is to contain the cost of a growing EDW by not just throwing all of the new data directly into it, but waiting until you know the data is useful for the masses. And the greatest benefit is that these environments provide the organization a very low-cost way to incubate innovative business strategies that often require massive volumes and varieties of data. The ultimate goal is to move only what is valuable to the relatively expensive EDW store, with no disruption to what's in place today.

3. Hadoop data platform as a basis for BI and analytics (Figure 5.7)

This third option is to make Hadoop the main store for all things related to business intelligence and analytics. EDW processes are untouched, but data flows are added to copy a lot of EDW data into Hadoop. This data is complemented with new data in Hadoop that never flows through the EDW. This can result in a reduction in the size of the EDW or simply a slowing of the growth and costs.

In this approach, the EDW can continue to support important operational tasks, like claims processing, and the majority

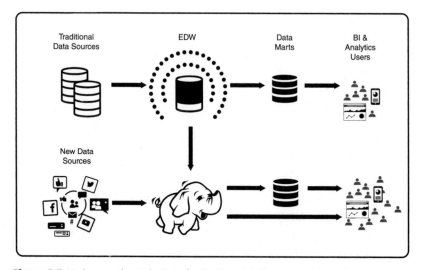

Figure 5.7 Hadoop as the Main Store for Business Intelligence and Analytics

of BI and analytics tasks can be moved to operate on the Hadoop store. Moving these processes to Hadoop lets us analyze greater volumes of data and receive more detail-level views than those in the EDW. Hadoop makes it possible to run reporting processes across huge volumes of data and to develop analytical models at a greater level of data granularity. Then, if necessary, these processes can be deployed into the EDW. Essentially, Hadoop becomes the single source for most users in this scenario.

Different models will work best for different organizations, but the great news is that the technology is flexible and agile enough to work with any type of existing database, providing healthcare organizations a great opportunity to establish big data analytics initiatives. With today's data volumes, it's impossible to ignore Hadoop, so it's certain that whichever option you choose for your big data analytics strategy, Hadoop will be a part of it!

Health Analytics

Now that we know what our infrastructure might look like, we can go back to talking about the analytics. In his book *Health Analytics* (Wiley: 2013), Jason Burke explains that the term *health analytics* can be used to describe the opportunity to embrace and prioritize information-based decisions that can transform healthcare into a collaborative, cost-aware, outcomes-oriented system. I agree with Jason and would add that it will also create opportunities to become consumer-centric.

Business Analytics and Clinical Analytics

Health analytics is commonly divided into two categories: business analytics and clinical analytics. Business analytics addresses the financial and operational aspects of healthcare, such as cost and utilization analyses, contract negotiations, and provider reimbursement. Clinical analytics, on the other hand, is focused on the care provided to patients and populations, and cover a range of analyses, such as risk stratification, population health, measuring intermediate and long-term outcomes, analyzing provider performance, and more.

While business and clinical analytics have different purposes, they overlap in many ways. For instance, it's impossible to understand the cost to a payer without understanding what level of care was provided, how many providers were involved, and what procedures took place. This interconnectivity is commonly referred to as the Iron Triangle of healthcare, in which the components of cost, quality, and accessibility are constantly in competition with one another. In other words, it's not possible to affect one aspect without affecting the other two aspects because the three are inextricable. This is one of the reasons why health analytics is critical; superior analytic tools are necessary to understand the complex interdependencies that drive medical outcomes and costs. And this analysis requires various big data from many different sources that must be integrated to complete the full picture of healthcare (Figure 5.8).

For example, the linking of claims data and clinical data has gotten a head start over recent years, and linking self-reported data, public health data, personal health statistics, and even nonhealth data, such as social media insights, is part of the evolution of big data analytics. The linking of various health data certainly has its challenges, from technicalities such as patient identification to security and regulative

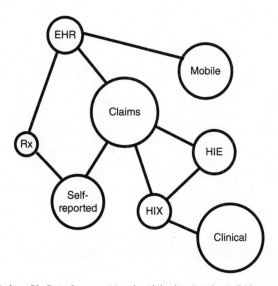

Figure 5.8 Various Big Data Sources Must be Linked to Get the Full Picture of Healthcare

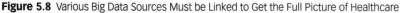

barriers, such as HIPAA and state legislation. However, healthcare decision makers are beginning to, and will need to, embrace new norms and innovative solutions for health data.

■ ■ ■

Let's look at some examples of different types of business and clinical analytics. The analytics maturity model in Figure 5.9 illustrates some ways that a healthcare payer organization—such as Blue Cross/Blue Shield, Medicaid, or Medicare—can use analytics. With analytics tools such as business intelligence, advanced data mining, predictive modeling, forecasting, and optimization, an organization can take their care delivery from the population level to a more personalized one, and from a reactive method to proactive methods focused on prevention, wellness, and, most important, the individual consumer.

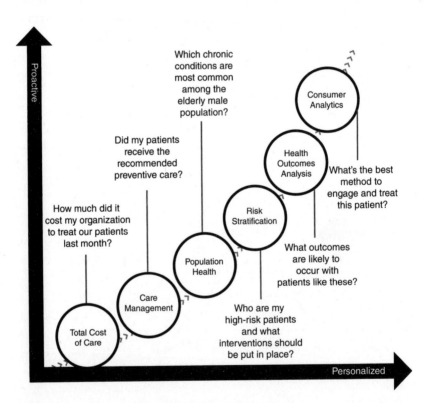

Figure 5.9 Example of a Healthcare Analytics Maturity Model

Let's imagine that we're a Medicaid agency that has built a data analytics infrastructure and is using the above model. We're starting by looking at our claims data, which gives us information on the cost and utilization of services, and we begin at the leftmost corner of the graph, with a broad population-level view of all of our Medicaid recipients. We start with descriptive analytics to look at the total cost of care: *How much is our agency spending on care?* We can capture an umbrella view of all of our costs within our system and can find age groups, disease groups, and other cohorts of individuals that contribute to the highest costs.

Then, we may start to look a little deeper, approaching care management goals. We want to use the data to identify which groups of people and which individuals are receiving the recommended preventive care. For example: *How many women are receiving their annual mammograms? How many diabetic patients are receiving their hemoglobin A1c (HbA1c) blood test at the recommended times?* At this point, we might decide to bring clinical data from electronic health records into our analysis to give us even more details on our diabetics. Clinical data combined with the claims data would let us see not only who's receiving their HbA1c tests, but also the results of their tests over time. This helps us understand the individual's health more precisely.

Moving on to the next bubble, population health, we decide that we want to learn more about our patient population with chronic conditions, and more specifically chronic pain. We want to see the groups of patients with chronic pain symptoms and what their outcomes are. Perhaps we start by looking at patients who have arthritis, and want to focus on individuals with osteoarthritis and rheumatoid arthritis. Using claims data to sort the patients with these diagnoses, we can see what treatments, follow-up visits, and therapies these individuals have had. We can also see the cost of these services: *How much are arthritic patients costing our organization?* Then, using our clinical data that we brought in, we can start to see more details about these patients, like their weight, blood pressure, and any clinical notes from their physicians. We may at this point decide to bring in self-generated data. Perhaps we've enrolled patients into mobile health programs, like Remedy, for instance. We can then look at how these individuals' pain is progressing each day. *Are the delivered treatments and medications helping patients in their daily lives? What trends are we seeing in the severity of pain? Are there improved outcomes and less pain? Are the number of doctors' visits reducing over time? Is the total cost of care being reduced over time?* We can also bring in text analytics to better understand unstructured data, like descriptions of pain that individuals have recorded through their mobile device. Building on all of these data points on cost, quality, and outcomes, we're starting to establish a 360-degree view of our individuals and of populations.

KICKING IT UP A NOTCH

This is a good time to start thinking about advanced analytics. While everything we've done so far has been insightful, we also need to look forward and learn what may happen in the future, using predictive and prescriptive analytics. The first part of our analytics journey was descriptive in nature; we analyzed what type of patients we have, what our cost breakdown is, and what types of treatments and services people are receiving. The next step of our journey is creating proactive, predictive, and personalized analytics. As we talked about earlier, the opportunity for these advanced analytics is ripe and the technology is there. As Farzad Mostashari, former ONC chief, pointed out at SAS's Healthcare Analytics Forum in 2014, "We have tools now we could only dream of before. We can now predict." We can predict ER visits, predict who will get sick and when, predict outbreaks across communities, and so much more. During his keynote, Mostashari drew an analogy of the use of predictive analytics by the Obama 2012 campaign[9] to healthcare, saying that in healthcare, every day is "model validation day"—election day. Every day someone gets sick, someone is diagnosed with cancer, someone has a heart attack; we have to put ourselves on the line and use prediction to optimize healthcare. Every other part of the economy does, and it's long overdue for healthcare to get on board.

Making Predictions

So then in our next stage of analysis—risk stratification—we can use predictive analytics to identify which patients are high-risk. Using the claims, clinical data, and mobile health data we've collected, we can create predictions on who may be at risk for a hospital admission or for developing a particular condition. This information not only will help us reach out to those individuals to offer preventive care, but it will help us to minimize potential costs down the road.

As we continue our journey toward being proactive and personalized, we can also use predictive analytics to analyze health outcomes. Let's say we've found some interesting groups of high-cost, high-risk patients and we want to analyze them more. We can pick certain groups of people of interest, for example, 29-year-olds with diabetes, and start to predict what types of outcomes we can expect. *Should we expect higher-than-average weight, or a comorbidity during a certain age range? What symptoms can we expect?* Utilizing all of the data, we're able to predict more precisely what the outcomes may be for certain groups and certain individuals. That helps us put the right interventions in place and treat these individuals more effectively to prevent a negative event from occurring.

Making Recommendations

We've approached the topmost corner of our bubble chart now, where there's increased personalization and proactivity. Here, the idea is to use analytics to engage the patient at a personal level to optimize health. Think back to machine learning and Netflix or Amazon; you know when you log on, and you're shown a variety of recommended shows and movies to watch or things to purchase? Similarly, in healthcare, we need recommendation engines that let healthcare payers and providers reach out to individuals in the best way to potentially change behavior. At this stage, bringing in social media data to understand an individual's behavior and lifestyle, and using behavioral analytics tools can help us build models on how best to reach out to individuals and learn what their likelihood of complying with a recommendation is. While these initiatives are new and require a lot of learning of individuals, the growth of self-generated data and social media data and machine learning is giving these efforts a boost.

BEHAVIORAL ANALYTICS

Behavioral analytics is a subset of advanced analytics that helps provide personalized guidance for consumers and is extremely valuable to both businesses and consumers. It's been used for a long time in the retail, ecommerce, and online gaming industries, and is proving itself to be extremely useful in healthcare, too.

Going back to the Amazon.com example, in which we talked about receiving personalized recommendations through recommendation engines, it's Amazon's use in this scenario of machine learning and behavioral analytics that makes it possible for the website to recommend additional products that customers are likely to buy based on their previous purchasing patterns on the site. Behavioral analytics is the part that captures information on how people behave on Amazon.com: What do they search for? How long do they stay on a page? What other items do they purchase? Machine learning is what lets this process scale up and automate; it learns all of these behaviors and gets smarter the more people use it. Together, it's a powerful combination.

■ ■ ■

Recall our discussion about sharing your personal health cloud with your team of providers. Sharing your health data with your providers gives providers an opportunity to use behavioral analytics to better monitor your health, reach out to you when there's a red flag, and keep up with your unique needs. For example, Ginger.io, a start-up company focused on improving mental health, provides behavioral analytics to providers so that they can deliver support to the right people at the right time. Through self-generated data and sensor data, their behavioral analytics engine helps providers better understand their patients' changing social, mental, and physical health status. For example, it may detect things like a low score on a mood survey, a concerning change in behavior patterns, or prolonged unresponsiveness. The system lets providers know immediately when an intervention can make a difference and can be most successful. It's a great way for providers to make real changes in their patients' behavior and to focus on wellness rather than just sickness.

For physicians taking on greater financial risk in a value-based payment environment, or getting reimbursed for non-face-to-face visits, these analytics are great news. More personalized analytics and access to self-generated, real-time information will be increasingly important for both health professionals as well as patients in the new health economy. And, it's not only a way for providers to increase their revenues, but also a way for individuals to be more incentivized to take care of themselves.

■ ■ ■

Well, there we have it: an analytics roadmap that utilizes a variety of tools and a variety of data to create new insights and foresights. I mentioned just a few things we could do, but there are virtually an infinite amount of things we could analyze, especially as new types of data are added. But the roadmap certainly doesn't end there, and we need to think further about personalization as we dive into consumer and behavioral analytics. As big data initiatives expand and the path to linking various types of health data becomes clearer, we're going to be able to obtain a broader and deeper view of patients and of their personal health. Additionally, with the growing amount of self-generated data, and with the critical need for better and more patient engagement, another area of analytics—personal health analytics—will be necessary in addition to business and clinical analytics.

PERSONAL HEALTH ANALYTICS

Earlier, we talked about personal health clouds and utilizing information to empower the patient. Patient empowerment and patient engagement require that we use *personal health analytics*. Personal health analytics is about *you* gaining insights on *your* health through *your* data. With the increased digitization of tracking and monitoring, most of us are collecting a wide range of information on ourselves— things that we may not even know are being tracked! This movement is often referred to as *quantified self*, or self-knowledge through self-tracking with technology. But, all of the things we track—calories, sleep, mood, weight, pain, and everything else that may be included in our personal health cloud—must all be analyzed for it to generate value back to us. That's why we need personal health analytics to create new information about ourselves that'll help us improve our health and well-being. We need to see relationships between the things we eat and the symptoms we have and the work we do; we need instant feedback on the fitness decisions we're making; we need alerts when we're at risk for an asthma attack. Right now, we ask our doctors when something goes wrong. But soon, our data will tell us before something goes wrong.

■ ■ ■

This evolution, while seemingly complex, is already beginning to emerge with the growth of personal health data, the soaring number of wearables and mobile health applications, and behavioral analytics. With these advances in technologies, the new era of personal health analytics will make personalized health more personal than ever imagined, strengthening the consumer–provider relationship and making it more collaborative. The analytics model we just went through will extend further with areas such as behavior change platforms and real-time feedback, and these new approaches will help us to solve a variety of cost issues related to personal behavior.

So many of today's health issues are related to personal behavior, and that's why personal health analytics is so important. Lots of studies on personal behaviors have emerged over the years, highlighting the growing importance of addressing these issues. According to Professor Ralph Keeney of Duke University, personal decisions are the leading cause of death, and through his research he's found that it's the decisions people make—to smoke, to eat poorly, to sit on the couch—that lead to diseases and in turn cause premature death.[10] It's estimated that the United States spends over $250 billion dollars a year in ER and doctor visits because 50 percent of patients forget to take their medications.[11] We also spend $50 billion trying to lose weight every year.[12] As big data analytics evolves to become more personalized, they'll help solve these detrimental behaviors—such as poor pill compliance and poor eating habits. For example, a smart watch may alert you to increase a dose of insulin today because of your diet patterns the last couple of days, or to bring your inhaler with you because the air quality is poor today, which often triggers your attacks. It's a great way for providers to make real change in their patients' behavior and focus on being proactive rather than reactive.

■ ■ ■

We ultimately want to be able to use data to generate optimal recommendations so that patients can make better decisions about their own health and so that healthcare providers can treat their patients more holistically and make the best decisions at the point-of-care. Providers, however, haven't traditionally been users of this type of data, and the immense amount of data that they could receive on all of their patients is overwhelming, to say the least. The new health economy encourages providers to look at data across their entire patient population, comparing themselves to other providers, and using health analytics to advance their value-based practice. If using data is perhaps the only way healthcare transformation will be successful, data consumption and usability are key. That's why we need visual analytics to consume and utilize data in everyday decision making.

VISUAL ANALYTICS

Visual analytics is an integrated approach that combines visualization, human factors, and data analysis.[13] The goal is to allow users to draw conclusions from data by representing information through human-centered, intuitive visualizations. It's much more than what meets the eye, though. Behind the scenes, it's the work of big data analytics that prepares and organizes massive amounts of data so that we can make sense of hundreds of thousands of variables. It's what makes visual interaction with big data possible so that we can pose known questions to the data and also explore the data for the unknown. Think about it as a playground for data where you can get your hands on billions of rows of data through simple visuals.

As we establish frameworks for health analytics, visual analytics is an essential piece of the big data analytics strategy. We need visualization to help democratize data to new users and make it accessible to everyone. At SAS, we created SAS Visual Analytics for this exact purpose, and it's a really neat way to see health data up close and personal. I'll give you a peek at it in what follows, and will show you more of visual analytics throughout the rest of the book.

Service Delivery

The new delivery models that are being established across the United States, such as accountable care organizations and patient-centered medical homes, rely on data and analytics to fulfill the goal of improved, coordinated care. This is the perfect scenario of where new users of data, such as primary care physicians, specialists, hospital administrators, and care managers, need to access and utilize large amounts of data—like claims, EHRs, and more. Unfortunately, a 2014 survey by NAACOS[14] found that for the early Medicare ACOs, learning to access and process data has been a significant challenge. More specifically, ACOs have been challenged with finding suitable software, building new skill sets to analyze data, and translating data into useful information for care managers and providers. This is a critical issue, because the access to and the usability of data analytics can make or break the success of an ACO.

Using visual analytics can help address these issues by changing the way ACOs approach data. Using visual analysis, providers can quickly get the unique population health insights they need from their data—such as performance measures, trends, costs, and outcomes— across multiple sites of care. And because it's simple and easy, providers can use these insights to improve decision making at the patient level. This isn't just a huge advancement for provider efficiency, but a game changer in making the ACO model successful. For example, the Institute of Health Policy and Practice (IHPP) at the University of New Hampshire uses visual analytics in conjunction with the state's all-payer claims database (APCD) to allow ACOs to see data and critical measures on their populations' health. They've created a Web portal with visual analytics through which the ACOs can use visualizations and interactive reports to better coordinate care. It's been so resourceful that it's replaced over 800 pages of documents!

Figure 5.10 shows an example of using visual analytics across a statewide all-payer claims database.

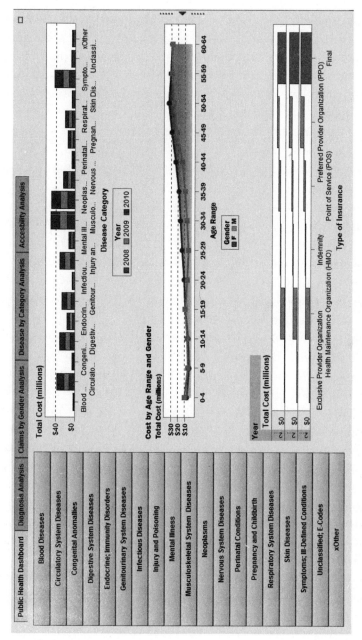

Figure 5.10 SAS Visual Analytics Report Created using a State All-payer Claims Database

Public Health

Another area of healthcare where visual analytics can be transformative is public health. Since the explosion of healthcare price
transparency dialogues a couple of years ago, huge volumes of data
are being collected and made available by the U.S. federal and state
governments. For example, healthcare.gov, healthdata.gov, data
.medicare.gov, and state APCDs are all sources of big data the public
sector is generating that can help guide policymaking. This data will
grow expeditiously as more states establish APCDs and the federal
and state-run insurance marketplaces continue generating new data
on individuals.

The use of these datasets remains challenging, and in general, the
databases are unexploited. Luckily, visual analytics brings a ton of possibilities to support public health and policymaking with all of this data.
For example, being able to visualize how disease is spreading across
communities, to predict outbreaks, to evaluate public health strategies, and in general provide policymakers with the ability to make
data-driven decisions is invaluable.

Figure 5.11 shows a report I created using SAS Visual Analytics
with the Medicare claims public use files.

Another good example of visual analytics for public health is the
monitoring of the spread of disease. The outbreak of the Zaire Ebola
virus in 2014, for example, quickly became a worldwide issue and
called for action by government and industry leaders as fast as possible. With such a deadly disease and a threat to societies around the
globe, we have to be able to stop Ebola and deliver information that
people can act on immediately. Imagine if we had the ability to visualize aggregated data on flu trends and disease trajectories and geospatial
information along with other data like passport records, financial transactions, and information gleaned from social networks. It's possible
that we could identify trends surrounding the virus and key elements
that would help us prevent its proliferation. Visualizing critical information within this data could change public health to be extremely
proactive and potentially save lives.

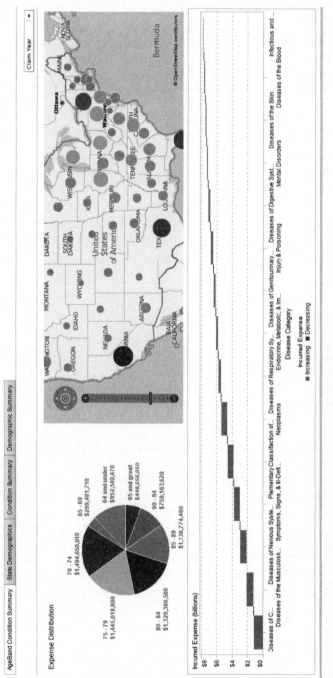

Figure 5.11 SAS Visual Analytics Report Created Using Medicare Claims Data

Other Health Research

For researchers doing all sorts of health studies, visual analytics can be used to explore various cohorts of individuals, for example, being able to visualize patients who have had certain sequences of events, such as a stroke, are on a common blood pressure medication, and are of similar age and weight. Furthermore, if we include social media data, we'll be able to analyze and visualize how medical trends are emerging and spreading. The possibilities are truly endless.

■ ■ ■

These examples of using visual analytics only scratch the surface of what it can offer in healthcare. As we continue to plunge into big data and transparency initiatives, it's critical that we find ways to synthesize big data for more human-centered insights; that's what will make big data a big success.

NOTES

1. http://www.juniperresearch.com/researchstore/key-vertical-markets/digital-health/monitoring-smart-accessories-ehr.
2. http://www.nihpromis.org/about/overview?AspxAutoDetectCookieSupport=1.
3. https://www.healthcatalyst.com/clinical-quality-improvement-in-healthcare.
4. https://www.abiresearch.com/press/more-than-30-billion-devices-will-wirelessly-conne/.
5. http://blogs.sas.com/content/corneroffice/2015/02/18/5-questions-to-prepare-you-for-the-internet-of-things/.
6. http://assets.fiercemarkets.com/public/healthit/kpmgannouncement.pdf.
7. http://blogs.sas.com/content/sascom/author/marktorr/.
8. https://en.wiktionary.org/wiki/data_lake.
9. http://www.nytimes.com/2013/06/23/magazine/the-obama-campaigns-digital-masterminds-cash-in.html?_r=0.
10. https://www.informs.org/content/download/255778/2414525/file/keeney.pdf.
11. http://lab.express-scripts.com/insights/industry-updates/~/media/b2d069aa4a2b4b188879a81ab0bab8aa.ashx.
12. http://money.usnews.com/money/personal-finance/articles/2013/01/02/the-heavy-price-of-losing-weight.
13. https://crawford.anu.edu.au/public_policy_community/content/doc/2008_Keim_Visual_analytics.pdf.
14. http://www.naacos.com/pdf/ACOSurveyFinal012114.pdf.

CHAPTER **6**

Implementation
Part 2

BACK TO THE BLUEPRINT

We've talked a lot about analytics now and have identified a lot of different areas in which analytics can help us. By now, you should have a pretty good idea of what health analytics is all about. Let's go back to the criteria we identified in Chapter 2. Remember, the whole purpose of human-centered design is to see issues through the customers' eyes and create solutions desirable to them. So it's important to always keep our customers, the consumers of the healthcare system, at top of mind.

The first two criteria we identified were motivation and adherence. How might we encourage individuals to be more motivated in achieving better health? And how might we ensure patient adherence to treatment plans?

Recall our findings from the blueprint: People lack motivation at all stages of healthcare; whether it's the motivation to go see a doctor, to stick to a treatment plan, or to follow up after a procedure, finding the motivation to engage with the healthcare system isn't something that comes naturally for many. And adhering to medications, meal plans, exercises, or other things can be even more challenging for many individuals. Think about the last time you tried changing a behavior or adopting a new habit. Maybe it was something like going for a run every morning, eating smaller portions, meditating, or just remembering to take your vitamins. You probably found that achieving long-term behavior change is an incredibly difficult task, despite our knowledge of the benefits.

We talked a bit about behavior change in our discussion about consumer analytics. Let's explore in more detail how big data analytics can help change behaviors.

CHANGING BEHAVIOR

By extending health insurance to millions of previously uninsured consumers, the U.S. ACA took a step toward behavior change, providing affordability, quality, and availability of private and public health insurance through federal and state marketplaces and Medicaid expansions. However, expanding health insurance is only a small piece of the pie. Just because consumers have better access to care doesn't mean that they'll actually seek care.

The healthcare ecosystem has to do more to support consumers in their attempts to embrace a sustained behavior change over the long term. With 75 percent of U.S. healthcare costs being spent on chronic disease, helping people manage issues over the long term is critical for better health outcomes and reduced costs. Detrimental issues like obesity, medication non-adherence, and smoking not only have negative impacts on health, but cost the healthcare system a fortune. Obesity results in an additional $190 billion a year in medical spending or 20 percent of U.S. healthcare expenditures, and one in three Americans is obese.[1] We all know people who've unsuccessfully tried to lose weight. In fact, there are upward of 108 million people on diets in the United States, and dieters typically make four to five attempts per year.[2] Smoking is no different. In 2011, 69 percent of adult smokers wanted to stop smoking and 43 percent had made an attempt to quit in the past year.[3] Unfortunately, many of these attempts are unsuccessful in creating a permanent change. Similarly, people have low adherence to prescription medications, and half of the annual prescriptions dispensed in the United States are not in fact taken as prescribed. The IMS Institute for Healthcare Informatics estimated that if we make improvements to medication adherence, we could potentially mitigate $105.4 billion in avoidable costs.[4]

These behaviors, and many others, create negative health outcomes and an outpouring of costs, and more needs to happen across the healthcare ecosystem to change them. It's an opportunity for technology and analytics to step up to the plate.

TOOLS FOR PROVIDERS AND PAYERS

For providers, assisting with behavior change has never really been a responsibility or incentive. For example, if a provider asks a patient to track his or her blood pressure daily, that doesn't mean that the provider will check in with the patient to make sure he or she is adhering to the request. Beyond the interaction during a face-to-face visit, there's little incentive to focus on the patient's long-term well-being. However, that's beginning to change. Providers are now being incentivized to support a patient's health journey beyond the office. And it's much needed to bring value and better total experiences to consumers.

I think that motivating providers to motivate their patients may work well if we use the right tools.

The Centers for Medicare and Medicaid Services (CMS) recently implemented the Chronic Care Management Services program, which reimburses providers for helping patients outside of the clinical setting. With the CCM program, providers will get paid for most of the things they can do for patients beyond the visit, things like performing medication reconciliation and overseeing the patient's self-management of medications; ensuring receipt of all recommended preventive services; and monitoring the patient's physical, mental, and social well-being.[5]

This gives providers the ability to get creative and find new approaches to support patients outside of the clinical setting. More specifically, it gives them an opportunity to use data and analytics to engage patients and support healthy behaviors while getting paid for it. It all comes at a great time, as we now have the incentives, the health analytics, and the technology to drive these improvements.

POPULATION HEALTH ANALYTICS

One way providers can be successful in the CCM program is through population health analytics (PHA). If you're in the healthcare industry, you know that the idea of managing population health is one of the most hyped opportunities in healthcare today; yet, I think it's fair to say, it's often misunderstood or not understood at all. Population health is about identifying those patients who have care gaps and would benefit most from additional support. It's also about providing targeted outreach to specific patients at the optimal time, which leverages behavioral analytics. PHA is key for sustained behavior change because, as we know, consumers need ongoing support outside the clinical setting.

My colleagues in the SAS Center for Health Analytics & Insights (CHAI) developed an eight-step approach for population health analytics, as shown in Figure 6.1. Let's discuss the eight steps and how they relate to behavior change.

The strategy begins with integrating data from diverse sources and preparing it for analysis, just like in the health analytics framework. This leads directly into assessing performance across the continuum

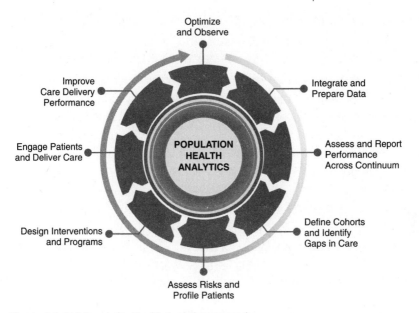

Optimize
and Observe

Improve
Care Delivery
Performance

Integrate and
Prepare Data

Engage Patients
and Deliver Care

**POPULATION
HEALTH
ANALYTICS**

Assess and Report
Performance
Across Continuum

Design Interventions
and Programs

Define Cohorts
and Identify
Gaps in Care

Assess Risks and
Profile Patients

Figure 6.1 SAS Population Health Analytics approach

of care. When we start reporting on performance system-wide, we inevitably find opportunities for improvement, whether they're high-cost or suboptimal outcomes. These opportunities require us to peel back successive layers of the onion and define increasingly granular cohorts of patients, ultimately ending with a population of one. Essentially, you keep peeling back more and more details until you reach one individual. Then, by understanding the needs and risks for each unique individual, providers can design interventions and tailor programs to engage each patient in a personalized care plan. Next, automation and workflow integration support the delivery of these interventions that are strategically designed to improve care coordination and performance. Last, by measuring the impact (success or failure) of each intervention, experimenting with new methods, and testing incremental quality improvements along the way, providers can learn and adapt to optimize the entire process.

Some of this probably sounds familiar from our previous health analytics discussion: creating a 360-degree view of the population by combining and organizing big data; then, risk-stratifying the populations to understand risk at both the cohort and individual patient levels; and finally, identifying unique interventions for specific patients to deliver the appropriate care. Using PHA, we can monitor patients' behavior over time to understand who responds to which interventions and to guide interventions in the future. Plus, it's a learning system. That means that the more data we have and the more we use the system, the more granular and accurate our predictions become.

Recall from our conversation on big data that nontraditional data, such as social media, consumer, survey, and environmental, along with our more traditional claims, clinical, pharmaceutical, biometric, and lab data, helps us establish a clearer 360-degree view of patients and populations. Additionally, new data types, such as streaming data from wearable and sensor devices, self-generated data from smartphone apps, text from blogs and forums, genomic data, and the digital output (audio and video) from telemedicine encounters, are all sources that will make population health a really powerful strategy. Further, using cloud analytics and big data platforms, we can expedite our PHA strategies.

■ ■ ■

For example, at SAS, we're working with Dignity Health, one of the largest health systems in the United States, to develop a cloud-based big data platform powered by a library of clinical, social, and behavioral analytics. Over time, the platform will connect and share data across the system's 39 hospitals and more than 9,000 affiliated providers. The goal is to help doctors, nurses, and other providers better understand patients and tailor their care for better outcomes and lower costs.

Similarly, Geneia, a population health management company, is using SAS to integrate disparate data sources, like EHR data, claims data, psychosocial data, activity tracker data, and device data, to create a comprehensive view of the patient both inside and outside the clinical setting. With this aggregated big data, they can support risk stratification of the patient population, allocate resources to close care gaps, and support behavior change.

With CMS's implementation of the Chronic Care Management program for Medicare and with the shift to value-based care, using population health analytics to drive behavior change will become an imperative. We'll also see many commercial health plans follow suit with new reimbursements in the future, making tools like population health analytics a necessity.

In fact, we're already seeing health plans using new types of data to support population health and to keep their consumers healthy, reduce costs, and decrease the number of office visits. With the rise in smartphone apps, wearables, and other digital sensors, health plans are encouraging members to track their health for a variety of purposes. Devices like Fitbit and Jawbone Up are starting to play a role in health insurance and how health plan costs are decided. Using this data to create more detailed risk profiles is already happening as well, and could escalate with the growth of digital health. That means real-time data on your health and wellness could impact your insurance rates, not just annually as usual, but as much as daily! Basically, the healthier you get the lower your premiums go.

This sounds kind of cool, but as you can imagine, there are implications there that could potentially create an unjust system. Some say it could create a two-tier system[6] where those who can afford the best health-tracking devices can ultimately get access to lower premiums. There also lies the risk that data could leak and be used by marketers to, for example, peddle diabetes medication or as extra fodder for insurers seeking to deny coverage. Pam Dixon, executive director of World Privacy Forum, says, "It's going to be very important that as we move toward the future we don't set up a system where people become pressured into wearing devices to monitor their health."[7]

That's why we need to be cautious about our strategies to drive behavior change. On the plus side, however, self-generated data on health and wellness can definitely help health plans to better identify outreach strategies, treatments, and coverage plans. Using a fair and effective population health analytics strategy, health plans can also successfully participate in the behavior change movement.

CONSUMER TOOLS

As health plans capture more information on consumers, consumers, too, will want more information on their health coverage options. With the health insurance marketplaces up and running, and the emergence of private health insurance exchanges, consumers now have new choices to make. Choosing a health plan isn't an easy task. How can we help consumers know what the best plan for them is, given their medical history, lifestyle, demographics, and general health needs?

If we can tailor health plan choices to match a unique individual's needs, we'll find more satisfied consumers and quite possibly more effective engagement with the healthcare system. That means we'll need predictive analytics like machine learning and recommendation engines that can predict and suggest the best options to individuals.

We've already started to see some efforts around this. For example, a start-up company, Picwell, has created a predictive recommendation engine that lets consumers quickly identify the best coverage options for them and their families. They use *de-identifiable* data on healthcare utilization, demographics, lifestyle, behavior patterns, financial information and networks, as well as consumer satisfaction to provide consumers with the plan options that are best for them. As the trend in improving the selection process advances, we'll likely see the addition of mobile health and wearable data that'll make these predictions even stronger. We talked earlier about health plans tapping into personal health data, creating more individualized health plan rates, but it could go much further than that. Health plans and insurance exchanges could actually use your personal health cloud data (by permission only), along with de-identifiable data of other individuals like you, to create uniquely personalized plans that may include personalized networks, wellness programs, and medication costs, all based on your projected needs and usage. As with all of our analytics discussions, though, privacy of the data is critical and consumers should have control over whether and which data is used for these purposes.

■ ■ ■

While all of this is exciting progress for behavior change, we need more direct-to-consumer tools to give behavior change the push it needs. We've talked about how healthcare providers and plans can use analytics to help their consumers change behaviors, and how personalization in health plans and the marketplaces can improve satisfaction. However, good health coverage, even if personalized to the nth degree, is only one step in encouraging more healthy behavior. We need consumer tools that will close the loop by providing personalized feedback and guidance.

My talented friend Lance wrote a really great piece on this topic in 2013, which is still really relevant today. He agreed to let me share it in this book. (Thank you, Lance, and nice job on being ahead of the curve!)

DESIGNING BEHAVIOR CHANGE

by Lance Cassidy

Can you remember the last time you successfully changed a behavior or adopted a new habit? Maybe it was something like going for a run every morning, meditating more, eating smaller portions, or just remembering to take your vitamins. As you might have found, achieving long-term behavior change is an incredibly difficult task, despite our knowledge of the benefits. Fortunately, there are a growing number of companies helping us take this on, particularly in healthcare. Companies like Fitbit, Myfitnesspal, and Runkeeper use sensors on our phones and wearable devices to track our behavior and display trending.

While these tools are certainly valuable and well-intentioned, people unfortunately tend to disengage with these kinds of tracking systems after the initial novelty wears off.

So then, what really changes our behavior for the long term? How might we keep people more engaged in their health long term by creating behavioral change systems that are proactive, personalized, and contextually aware?

Current Tracking Systems

Let's say you decide you want to start tracking your diet or activity level in hopes of making healthier decisions. You could start by browsing the 20,000+ apps in the iTunes store under "Health and Fitness," or you could go with one of the more popular health tracking systems like Fitbit. Let's use Fitbit's Aria smart scale as an example, because it's one of the simpler tracking systems. Every time you step on the smart scale it records your weight and body fat percentage and automatically syncs this data with a smartphone app. You can then view your progress with beautiful charts and graphs and see if you're losing or gaining weight. The assumption is that you'll make healthier decisions because you can see trending and progress. However, the reality is that these tracking systems tend to become more of a diary of failures than a tool to help you achieve long-term wellness. This is because long-term behavior change requires more than the knowledge of the impact of your past behaviors. It's like an open-loop problem, where the connection to future behavior is the missing link.

This is a very real problem for companies selling behavioral tracking systems. The Quantified Self movement won't graduate into the mainstream until people know what real-life impact they can achieve with the data. Our guess is that this is why people who start using this kind of tracking software tend to slowly disengage after the initial novelty wears off. At a Startup Weekend in Raleigh, NC, we interviewed 24 people on the street who had used some sort of tracking system and found that 80 percent of them had discontinued long-term use. Participants who had discontinued use were not really able to say why; they either learned what they wanted to know from the data or they just stopped using it.

This isn't to say that tracking systems aren't useful. If a person already has a healthy behavior established, like running every day, then tracking systems can optimize that behavior. For example, Nike Plus uses GPS and motion sensing from your phone to give information about your run. You can see how many calories you burned, see the distance you traveled, and even share a map of your run on social networks for more encouragement. This feedback might make you run a little more, or at least remind you how awesome you are, which is great. But that just validates my thought that tracking systems are most valuable for people who already have a behavior established, not necessarily for people interested in adopting a new habit. In order to achieve long-term behavior change, we need to think much deeper about what factors influence behavior change in the real world. Current health tracking applications are all about showing you how many steps you just walked or how many calories you just ate, not about suggesting what you should do in the future. What we really want to know is how far we *should* walk, or what we *should* eat. This is the leap I call moving from tracking behavior to *guiding* behavior.

From Tracking to Guiding Behavior

Guiding behavior is a much more complex task because it requires us to be proactive about how we communicate to the end-user. First, we need extremely low-effort ways to collect data. This is a problem that many tracking systems have solved—collecting data through mobile devices, wearables, or quick self-logging. The difficult part is then synthesizing this data and using analytics to build an algorithm for recommending the next most desirable action. Next, we need to be able to communicate this recommendation in the most compelling way by having a much deeper understanding of context, personal preferences, and timing. Finally, we need a way to measure the effectiveness of this communication so that we can make smarter communications in the future, effectively closing the behavioral guidance loop. Luckily, clinical psychologists, cognitive psychologists, and behavioral economists have already made great progress building frameworks for behavior change. We can now use these frameworks and apply them within the mobile context with the goal of automating behavior change.

Dr. B.J. Fogg, a professor at Stanford's Persuasive Technology Lab (http://captology .stanford.edu/), has established three principal factors that need to occur in order for a target behavior to happen. The user must have sufficient motivation, ability, and an effective trigger all at the same instant. The third factor, an effective trigger, is a big chunk of what's missing from tracking systems. A trigger could be something simple like a sound, a vibration, a text message, a color change, or something more elaborate—like an email to your spouse notifying him or her that you forgot to take your medication. Whatever the case, the user needs to notice the trigger, associate that trigger with the target behavior, and have sufficient motivation and ability to complete the target behavior.

It all boils down to the fact that what motivates people to change varies greatly by individual, and that's why personalization in behavioral guidance systems is so important. Some people are competitive, some people need positive encouragement, some people like games, and some people just want to be told what to do.

The timing of a trigger is equally important. It must occur at the most opportune moment to push the user past his activation threshold. For example, let's say we want to help individuals make in-the-moment decisions about their diet. We can use the user's health goals, historic calorie information, food preferences, and GPS location to understand what restaurant he's at and proactively recommend what's most healthy to order. For example, "Hey Lance, Try the black bean burrito" (Figure 6.2).

Taking it further, let's say the person later goes to the gym; his smartphone could alert him of how much more activity is required to burn off the food that he previously ate. Something like, "Hey Lance, Bike for 10 more minutes to burn off the burrito!" (Figure 6.3).

Figure 6.2 Personalized Alert on a Smart Watch

Figure 6.3 Personalized Alert on a Smartphone

These are just a couple of examples that merely scratch the surface. There's massive amounts of data that can be used to create personalized behavior guidance systems. Electronic health records, personal preferences, habits on social media, and other data collected from mobile devices and wearables can all be utilized. The important thing is to start turning our heads from gathering and synthesizing data to figuring out how the data can help make a change. If we can figure out how to effectively change people's behavior, even by just a small percent, the impact it'll have on everyone will be massive. Think about how much detrimental behaviors like poor pill compliance and poor diet habits impact us, and society.

The United States spends $258 billion a year in ER and doctor visits because 50 percent of patients forget to take their medications. The United States also spends $50 billion trying to lose weight every year. That's why building effective behavior change platforms aren't just interesting business opportunities for brands to interact with people's lives; it affects the entirety of society. And everything boils down to the little behaviors we engage in every day. Our daily behaviors define who we are, our levels of happiness, our health, and our fulfillment in our lives. We don't really think about it, but we are a culmination of habits that are accumulated over time. If we can create platforms that allow us to be more intentional about the habits we introduce into our lives, then we can build products that are truly life-changing.

Take a moment to think about tracking versus guiding—what examples can you come up with in addition to the ones shown in the table?

Tracking	Guiding
Meals	Automated meal plan creation: ■ Shopping lists and costs ■ Recipes
Workouts	Weekly workout schedules: ■ Integrated with work and personal calendar
Calories	Meals + exercise suggestions: ■ Goal-based
Mood	Interactive recommendations: ■ Meditations ■ Games
Pain	Alerts for stretch breaks: ■ Videos of stretching exercises

I like Lance's article because it puts a lot of what I've discussed so far into the consumer perspective, everything from the 360-degree view of consumers to predictive analytics, personal health clouds, and behavioral analytics. And it all boils down to one thing: creating healthy behaviors. If we can *guide* behavior, we can be really successful in creating radical change. When that happens throughout the healthcare system, healthcare will have its role in the transformation economy.

CONSUMER CHOICE AND TRANSPARENCY

Data *Liberación!*

This signature phrase by Todd Park, former U.S. White House chief technology officer, epitomizes the revolution that's been taking place at both the national and state level in the area of healthcare transparency. The slogan was first coined in 2010, and it expressed Park's entrepreneurial vision to open huge amounts of health data to the public for the purposes of sharing, collaborating, and innovating. At the federal level it led to initiatives like OpenData.gov, HealthData.gov, and Health Datapalooza. And at other levels of government and across the private sector, the implications of "data *liberación*" have generated a lot of positive discussion around data democratization, becoming the new mantra for many organizations nationwide.

Todd Park pointed out there are large amounts of data in the federal Department of Health and Human Services on the health of communities and the quality of healthcare providers, and information about drugs and charges to Medicare.[8] He advocated for sharing these datasets to facilitate innovation in healthcare and advance U.S. efforts in achieving the Triple Aim (improving the patient experience of care, improving the health of populations, and reducing the per-capita cost of healthcare). In 2013, we saw Park's vision come to significant fruition with many of these aforementioned datasets revealed to the public.

Parallel to these discussions about data democratization, state governments have also been figuring out how to make their respective healthcare delivery systems more transparent. Bringing transparency to healthcare data is challenging to states for many reasons: obtaining stakeholder support and garnering the necessary funds and ensuring the security and privacy of individuals, to name a few. However, a lot of progress has been made and continues to be made by many states.

One initiative that's gained significant momentum in the area of healthcare transparency is the creation of *all-payer claims databases* (APCDs). An APCD is a database typically created from a state mandate that generally includes data derived from medical claims, pharmacy claims, eligibility files, provider (physician and facility) files, and dental claims from a state's private and public payers.[9] The first APCDs appeared in the Northeast, beginning with Maine in 2003, and gained rapid regional adoption thereafter. States are adopting APCD policies with the intent of bringing transparency across the entire spectrum of healthcare delivery, to in turn promote more informed decision making. I got the opportunity at SAS to work on these initiatives with states and quickly found that the potential for these types of databases is huge.

Data transparency opens up a realm of possibilities for everyone in the healthcare ecosystem. APCDs aren't only a solution for transparency, but are actually a platform for both transparency and innovation, and states should continue to embrace this initiative as the data *liberación* movement unfolds.

WHERE WILL TRANSPARENCY LEAD US?

Stakeholders across the healthcare system are agreeing that success-ful reform will depend on our ability to gather, share, and analyze healthcare data in a consumable manner. The idea that we can't man-age what we can't measure is becoming more evident as the issue of transparency—or lack thereof—is debated across the country.

A major step toward healthcare transparency was the Centers for Medicaid and Medicare Services' (CMS) release of Medicare provider charge data in 2013, which at first comprised Medicare inpatient hospital charges for 100 of the most common inpatient diagnoses. A subsequent dataset reflected outpatient charge data for 30 of the most common ambulatory payment codes. Other activities also emerged in parallel, such as $87 million in grant money for states to support rate review and increase price transparency. A year later, in April 2014, CMS released new data on medical services and procedures furnished to Medicare fee-for-service beneficiaries by physicians and other healthcare professionals. For the first time, a look into how physicians practice in the Medicare program was made possible. Most recently, at the 2015 Health Datapalooza, CMS announced its third release of Medicare hospital utilization and payment data. With this release also came an announcement by CMS's acting administrator, Andy Slavitt, to open up the data to the private sector to "shake up healthcare innovation and set a new standard for data transparency." Historically, CMS hasn't given access to researchers and private industry if they intended to use it to develop products or tools to sell. But times are changing and the intent of this decision is to do exactly that—spur the development of new technologies and innovations. I love it.

As for the state governments, they've been taking advantage of grant monies through the pursuit of transparency initiatives like APCDs and data centers. Other groups, like the Health Care Cost Institute (HCCI), are aggregating claims data from many sources to promote independent research on price variation around the nation. Even large pharmaceutical companies like GlaxoSmithKline are joining the transparency movement by contributing anonymized clinical trial data into a globally accessible cloud environment.

Lots of unprecedented activity in transparency is taking place across the industry, and these pursuits aren't ill founded. In 2013, the *New York Times* published a compelling piece on price variations for common procedures around the world and stated, "In many other countries, price lists of common procedures are publicly available in every clinic and office. Here, it can be nearly impossible to find out."[10] In fact, 29 states actually received a failing grade in healthcare price transparency in a study released in 2013 by the Healthcare Incentives Improvements Institute (HCI3) and the Catalyst for Payment Reform.[11] Only two states, Massachusetts and New Hampshire, received A grades; both of these states operate APCDs.

In 2014, the results improved slightly, and quality transparency was added as part of the study. Information on the quality of providers is equally important in helping consumers make informed decisions, but, unfortunately, the majority of states failed this test as well. In the 2015 report, again, little progress was made, and the results showed that 90 percent of states still fail to provide adequate price information to consumers.[12]

■ ■ ■

Why all this noise and attention on transparency? Why does the U.S. healthcare system need it, and, more important, what does it mean for the consumer? While transparency in healthcare has many advantages, there are three core benefits that can enable better health outcomes and increased value for consumers.

1. *Consumer choice.* Going back to our criteria, we identified choice as one of the main things that healthcare consumers desire: How might we create more opportunities for choice within the healthcare system? Consumers want to choose their own doctors, have a say in their treatments, know up front how much a visit or procedure will cost them, and be informed about various other choices they make regarding the cost and quality of their care. Consumer choice is vital in every market but, as we discovered, lacking in healthcare. Recently, many people have been comparing the purchasing of healthcare services to purchasing a new car. They say that you wouldn't buy a car without knowing its price or level of quality, so why is

it that we make important decisions about our health without cost and quality information? That's a good question.

When consumers have the information they need, they can make better-informed decisions about the services they receive. This can change incentives across the board as healthcare payers and providers are faced with more competition. For example, after New York State began publishing outcomes data for coronary artery bypass grafting (CABG) in 1989, the state's CABG mortality rates fell by more than 40 percent; furthermore, the hospitals with better outcomes saw growth in their market shares.[13]

2. *More accountability.* Transparency also makes healthcare stakeholders more accountable for their actions. For example, with more data available, states can identify if a particular hospital has unusual mortality rates or if a Medicaid managed care entity is providing the required preventive care to its members.

3. *Better performance.* Last, but not least, transparency drives performance. Imagine as a student in high school, your test grades were posted publicly for everyone to see and you continuously received one of the poorest grades in the class. What would you do about it? Studies have shown that the possible scrutiny by peers is sufficient on its own to promote behavior change.[14] And chances are no medical provider wants to be known as having the poorest grades in the class.

Many other benefits can stem from the three above if transparency is delivered to the right people in a consumable way. Perhaps most important, transparency opens opportunities for innovation across all facets of the healthcare system. As states establish APCDs, these repositories will serve as opportune platforms for creating both transparency and innovation.

WHAT IS AN APCD?

All-payer claims databases are state-mandated repositories that collect healthcare claims data from all healthcare payers in a state, including both private and public payers. Additionally, APCDs generally collect

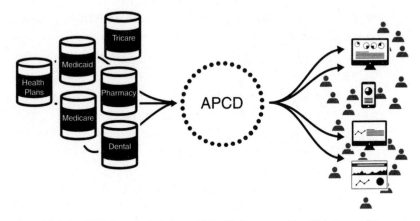

Figure 6.4 An APCD Collects Data from All Health Payers and Is a Rich Source for Reporting and Analysis

pharmacy and dental claims. The database provides a unique opportunity to obtain a detailed view of how healthcare costs are dispersed across a state, allowing a variety of reporting and analysis to be done on this rich data. This is illustrated in Figure 6.4.

An amplified interest in APCDs has been led by the transparency debate, and many states are pursuing the APCD effort with the intent of empowering consumers to understand, prior to receiving a healthcare service, its estimated price and how it could vary by healthcare provider.[15] With such a large number of employers (32%) considering high-deductible health plans as the only benefit option to employees, and 22 percent of all employers now offering high-deductible health plans as the lone benefit option for employees,[16] the information on price is becoming more and more critical for consumers.

WHAT'S THE LANDSCAPE?

After the initial wave of APCD implementations in the Northeast region between 2003 and 2008, many other states began to introduce legislation or establish a voluntary or multi payer effort. The year 2013 was an eventful one for APCDs due to federal grant monies like the CMS Innovation Awards, the Health Insurance Exchange establishment grants, and $87 million in grants for price transparency and rate review. These funding sources, combined with the increasing demand for transparency, have resulted in many more legislators and policymakers considering the creation of an APCD in their states. The interest in APCDs is undoubtedly escalating at a rapid speed.

Today, 16 states already have an existing APCD or a voluntary multi payer database, according to the APCD Council (Figure 6.5). In fact, all others but ten have a strong interest in an APCD or are currently implementing one. States such as Arkansas, Nebraska, and New York have already initiated planning, legislative, and/or procurement activities. In the state of Washington, Governor Jay Inslee signed legislation in May 2015 to establish a fully functional APCD, and in Kentucky, the Foundation for a Healthy Kentucky has been advocating for one in their state since 2014. States with existing APCDs are making progress by releasing data to more users and expanding their use of the data with advanced analytics.

APCD as a Platform for Innovation

Knowing is not enough; we must apply. Willing is not enough; we must do.

—Johann Wolfgang von Goethe

Establishing an APCD and providing consumers access to it is simply the first step in reaping the benefits of this data. The true benefits of the APCD extend well beyond consumer access and transparency; they're found in the widespread dissemination and analysis of the data by healthcare decision makers. It's when the data is used for decision making that we see initiatives like consumer behavior change, cost containment, and quality improvement efforts come to fruition. The potential users of an APCD are many, and the use cases are virtually boundless (Figure 6.6). I've provided just a few in Table 6.1.

There are so many possibilities for utilizing APCD data in creative ways, and as APCDs mature and are expanded to bring in other data, like clinical, financial, and public health, even more ways to analyze this data will be revealed. With links to health information exchanges (HIE), health insurance exchanges (HIX), and other sources, APCDs have the opportunity to provide a true 360-degree view of healthcare delivery to the entire healthcare system (Figure 6.7).

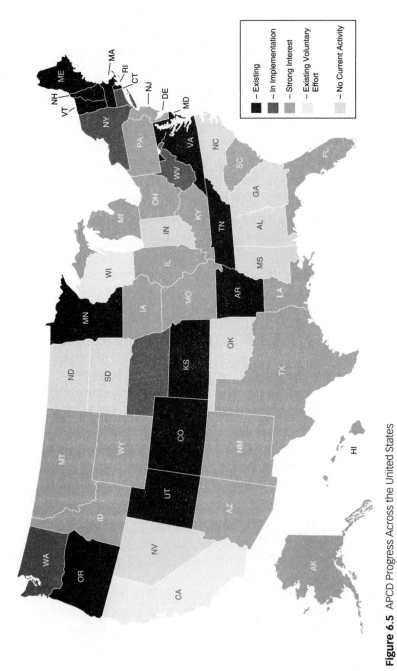

Figure 6.5 APCD Progress Across the United States

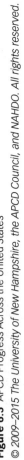

Table 6.1 APCD Users and Use Cases

Public Health	▪ Discover the needs of populations and communities to align public health initiatives more effectively. ▪ Identify communities that provide cost-effective care and promote similar practices across the state. ▪ Forecast population health and disease prevalence to implement prevention and education programs.
Health Plans	▪ Discover high-quality, low-cost treatments to refine provider reimbursement models. ▪ Analyze episodes of care and their associated costs and understand how they compare to other plans. ▪ Evaluate claims history information for new populations to inform expansion into different geographic areas. ▪ Identify current and future health needs in a geographic location and modify contracts with providers accordingly. ▪ Target populations best suited for accountable care organizations and patient-centered medical homes to reduce long-term costs.
Providers	▪ Strengthen quality measurement by benchmarking performance against peers on a variety of metrics. ▪ Identify health status of the population served to provide more targeted care. ▪ Obtain a holistic view of an individual's services to create seamless care transitions. ▪ Assist clinicians in providing the best possible care for individual patients, informed by evidence-based data. ▪ Enable providers to understand and manage new care models such as episodic or accountable care.
Employers	▪ Select providers and design insurance products based on quality, cost, and efficiency. ▪ Examine how the benefits and premiums compare with those of other employers. ▪ Obtain information useful for rate negotiation and benefit changes.
Researchers	▪ Evaluate cost, quality, access, utilization, and patient satisfaction indicators across different payment and delivery models, geographic areas, and populations to inform and influence policymaking. ▪ Analyze treatment options across variables such as age, gender, and ethnicity and identify disparities.

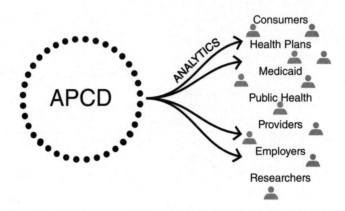

Figure 6.6 Potential Users of an APCD Are Many, and the Use Cases Are Virtually Boundless

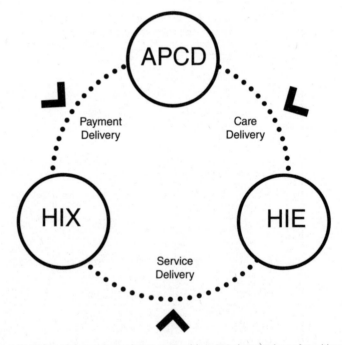

Figure 6.7 APCDs Link to HIEs and HIXs to Provide a 360-degree View of Healthcare Delivery

THE KEY TO SUCCESS: BIG DATA ANALYTICS

The APCD certainly fits the mold of big data and it's evident that the essential driver in making APCDs a platform for transparency and innovation will be the analysis of the data that resides in them. Providing the right users access to large amounts of data—in a consumable manner with the ability to analyze it in unique ways—will elevate transparency and innovation. That's why APCDs will be reliant on the appropriate state health IT infrastructures. As I talked about earlier, traditional systems for managing health data were transactional in nature, storing mountains of data often without use; robust APCDs, on the contrary, require modern systems that focus on quickly making the data useful to a wide variety of users.

These next-generation APCDs will require high-performance computing with the ability to deliver the insight and foresight stakeholders need to improve health outcomes and reduce healthcare costs. APCD infrastructure must also be flexible and scalable: flexible to allow seamless transitions from other systems and databases and cooperation with new platforms, and scalable to facilitate the growth of data and the addition of different types of data over time. APCDs also will require a wide array of functionality to accommodate consumer portals, predictive analytics, user experience, data visualization, and more. In fact, all of the big data and analytics tools that we've discussed so far can be leveraged within an APCD, as it can essentially be a health data cloud of its own with the right tools like Hadoop and cloud analytics. Everything from business and operational analytics, to clinical, behavioral, and personal health analytics can be built off of an APCD, and these are the functions that'll be critical to APCDs delivering value.

So as states design APCDs, they should do so with analytics in mind. The conversations today shouldn't be about the big data that makes up an APCD, but about the big data analytics that is made possible through the database. Furthermore, they shouldn't be about the long road to analytics, but rather about creating systems that will *let us do analytics now*.

ESTABLISHING AN APCD

We should not oversell transparency as a panacea. But it must become the defining characteristic of the NHS: the future must be open.
—Tim Kelsey, NHS Commissioning Board[17]

In 2010, the U.K.'s National Health Service (NHS) embarked upon a bold journey to bring transparency to its citizens. Prime Minister David Cameron pledged that the NHS will make comparative performance and prescribing data for individual primary care practices, as well as anonymized patient-level data, publicly available to permit scrutiny of clinical teams in hospitals.[18] Additionally, the NHS made plans to digitize all health data and make it available to staff by April 2018.

The introduction of transparency as the new norm didn't come easy in the U.K., and as the United States travels down a similar road, states and other stakeholders in the healthcare system will be faced with many of the same challenges that the U.K. faced and continues to face.

To make the journey easier, I'm providing some considerations based on case studies of past implementations. Whereas I talk about them as they relate to an APCD, they're all relevant across any big data and health analytics strategy, and I'll throw in some non-APCD examples as well. My suggestions are to:

- Get started with the data you have.
- Recruit political support.
- Deliver value and privacy to consumers.
- Involve the healthcare community.

Get Started with the Data You Have

If states wait for perfect data, they'll likely never get started on any transparency initiative. They have to start somewhere to begin addressing the unavoidable issue. Many states worry about the inconsistency or poor quality of claims data, but healthcare claims are the most structured and the most accessible data in the United States, making it a great place to start. Inaction creates no incentives for improving the quality of data, and introducing transparency may in fact be the only way to actually improve data quality and help establish better standards. In fact, the NHS found that making anonymized data publicly available improved coding accuracy in the U.K. dramatically.

It's important to start small with both APCD data collection and analytics. Legislation for claims collection isn't typically an easy task so some states have taken incremental steps toward a full-scale APCD. For example, Washington and Oregon started with a voluntary payer database, and in 2012 three health plans in California launched an effort to pool their claims together. While not perfect, voluntary and multi payer efforts provide a great start.

Regarding analytics, APCDs offer a grand opportunity to find patterns and trends, create forecasts, identify correlations, and do other types of analyses to help consumers and to inform the present and future of a state's population health. Some states, like Massachusetts and New Hampshire, are finding success using advanced analytics tools to perform a variety of analyses on their data. Other states haven't yet identified how they will utilize the data in their APCDs. Start small and at the beginning of the analytics life cycle, and let these activities mature as stakeholders in the healthcare system deem appropriate. Once stakeholders see the value of analyzing this rich data, the analytics will scale naturally.

The critical part is that stakeholders and steering committees for the APCD build a vision for analytics early on and don't leave analytics out of consideration when implementing these systems. There's a path to analytics no matter what the infrastructure and data look like. It might be a Hadoop database, or a fast, software-as-a-service deployment, or a full-scale high-performance analytics installation. Regardless of the path, analytics is how these big health data efforts will truly provide value.

Recruit Political Support

In order for transparency to be effective, it has to be supported at the top levels of government. Policymakers must work actively toward garnering the necessary support when introducing the idea of an

APCD. Many legislators have been successful or are currently working on this effort. For example, Delegate John O'Bannon III helped push the APCD legislation along in Virginia, and the state recently established its database. In Washington State, Governor Jay Inslee led the effort in 2015, making the following statement.

> Last year there was a lot of disagreement about the All Payer Claims Database. While the information collected in the database can significantly help us improve the quality and cost of healthcare, there were important differences of opinion to work out. This year, the different groups came together—my office, insurers, providers, advocates, the Washington Health Alliance, small and large businesses and local governments—and worked constructively to resolve their issues. The people of the state are the winners. Quality and cost information are now going to be available to all of us.

Policymakers can use the success of other state APCDs, the availability of funding, and the bipartisan nature of the APCD policy to help advocate for data transparency policies and to gain the required backing for the project. Some things are just good policy, and many would agree that APCD is one of those things.

Deliver Value and Privacy to Consumers

Naturally the public will have concerns about the possible exposure of health data. Protections to secure private data should be addressed early and often in the planning and implementation stages. In addition, states should be very proactive in ensuring and conveying that the privacy and security of personal health information is a high priority. We've discussed privacy and security several times now, and it can't be emphasized enough. Ensuring that regulations for data sharing are put in place early on is critical for all big data efforts, and even more so in healthcare, given the sensitivity of data. Figuring this out in the initial stages will generate credibility and support among consumers.

The quicker a state can show value to consumers, the more support it'll receive from stakeholders. It all boils down to what value the

APCD, or any other healthcare data initiative, provides to the recipient of healthcare services—the consumer.

Colorado, for example, garnered a substantial amount of consumer support of its APCD after creating an interactive public interface of key healthcare measures. The portal provides many benefits to Colorado citizens and continues to receive positive opinions nationwide. If a state can show value early on, with access to usable, meaningful information through portals and apps, for example, consumers will have a better understanding of how their data is being used and protected. Garnering this consumer support will pave the way for future innovations.

Involve the Healthcare Community

McKinsey & Company found that perhaps the most important lesson the NHS learned through its transparency efforts is that any attempt to introduce transparency will be sustainable only if frontline healthcare professionals understand the benefits of the effort.[19] Healthcare professionals must also be involved in designing the program's implementation. In the U.K., for example, clinicians led the effort to identify which key metrics would be assessed first.

All healthcare system stakeholders need to be engaged when establishing an APCD in order to make it a sustainable and rewarding benefit to society. It's vital to seek feedback from contributors and users of the APCD, such as payers, providers, and researchers. For example, in Connecticut, both the Connecticut Hospital Association and the Connecticut Association of Health Plans supported the state's efforts to implement an APCD. Keith Stover, spokesman for the Connecticut Association of Health Plans, stated, "We have been actively engaged in the planning and development of the APCD since the very first meeting and have been working closely with the technical folks involved to make sure that it will work and that the information is useful and usable." This participation is essential and a best practice in APCD deployment.

The state of New York is another example of effective participation by professional organizations. Since its initial APCD planning stages, New York has been proactive in bringing together representatives from health plans, provider organizations, researchers, and other interest groups to participate on the state's APCD steering committee. Additionally, the New York State Department of Health (NYS DOH) continually informs stakeholders of progress through a variety of channels. As a result, the NY DOH has put together an extensive collection of APCD use cases that illustrates the benefits of the APCD for all stakeholders of the healthcare system. Moreover, the organization has outlined a notable vision for its APCD, touching on topics such as HIE and public health integration and the utilization of the APCD in its broader health reform efforts.

WHY APCDS?

I like the APCD concept because it has the potential to address many of the issues that consumers and all other stakeholders in the healthcare system encounter. Plus, it has a defined starting point (with claims data), and a regulatory force to ensure large participation. Whether it's adding new types of data or new types of analytics, the value that we can get from it, or any other similar initiative, is beneficial to everyone.

■ ■ ■

While all these possibilities to use APCDs sound valuable and achievable, and even though several states have created one, we unfortunately, have yet to see the true potential of these databases. This seems ironic, but although the premise of the APCD is to create healthcare data transparency, many APCDs have stringent data release rules that in some cases allow only the managing entity to have access (#notverytransparent). The transparency necessary for analytics and innovation won't happen without, well, making the data transparent.

So, ensure privacy, but free the data! We need the healthcare community, the non-healthcare community, individuals, and entrepreneurs exploiting these and other databases to generate value in our healthcare system. Through activities like hack-a-thons, datapaloozas, and start-up weekends we can find new ways to leverage the data and build more use cases for all the interested parties, especially consumers. Consumer web portals could turn into mobile apps to search for plans and providers; patient portals could be created with an individual's' claim history; recommendation engines could provide consumers with recommendations for health plans based on their history; personal health records could be created with claims, HIE, and HIX data; and all these things could even be pushed to a personal health cloud, all accessible by a mobile device. The key is liberating the data, or as Todd Park would say, "data *liberación.*"

CLINICAL TRIAL DATA TRANSPARENCY

A good example of data transparency done right is something called *clinical trial data transparency* (CTDT). Over the last couple of years, I've seen this groundbreaking project take shape, and it's made huge strides for the broader healthcare and life sciences industries. In a nutshell, CTDT is about pooling together anonymized patient-level clinical trial data into a globally accessible cloud. The cloud is available to researchers and others in the scientific community to learn from all of this data and advance medical knowledge. SAS started its Clinical Trial Data Transparency project with GlaxoSmithKline in 2013, and quickly after, lots of other pharmaceutical companies followed suit. It's kind of a big deal. Imagine having access to all of this clinical trial data from multiple companies all in a single place. Pharmaceutical companies spend millions of dollars gathering this data throughout clinical trials and the data is rich and incredibly useful in finding new discoveries about medicine. It's good for science, good for business, and good for a humanity initiative that, in a very short timeframe, has come together at very large scale.

But clinical trial data transparency isn't all that different from the APCD world, in that it wasn't easy to liberate this data and garner the necessary support. In fact, the idea of it wasn't initially embraced, but despite that, the concept was able to quickly become a reality. Stakeholders in the industry took the right steps to get there; they identified security and privacy as an utmost priority, collaborated with the broader industry to work as a team, created governance systems for the use of the data, and, most important, they used modern technologies that allowed them to build a secure repository with built-in analytics. Built-in analytics ensure that researchers can make the best use of this data, and of course, generate more interest in accessing the cloud. But above all, it makes the liberation of data a success. I think that creating the cloud with the utility of the data at top of mind helped make CTDT a successful data transparency initiative from the get-go. The contributors of the data and the industry as a whole have gone from the notion of "How do we think this could work?" to "How is it working?" and "How can we improve this?" really rapidly. The swiftness of the effort as well as the ability to create shared goals for data transparency globally are really commendable. If we could bring this concept into healthcare at the same level of agility as the life sciences industry has done, we'd have ourselves a big data analytics blockbuster.

The same type of rapid transparency and innovation is what we need to extend and accelerate our healthcare transparency efforts, and at the core lies the fact that price and quality transparency are needed to change the incentives throughout the healthcare system. It's not just a wish, but rather an imperative and necessary foundation for other health initiatives. State governments are a critical component of this movement and can make a significant impact by creating all-payer claims databases and using big data analytics. Although healthcare transparency initiatives and processes will vary from state to state based on political backing, stakeholder support, funding, and more, if all states start small, we can make a difference in our nation's healthcare system.

NOTES

1. http://www.reuters.com/article/2012/04/30/us-obesity-idUSBRE83T0C8201 20430.
2. http://abcnews.go.com/Health/100-million-dieters-20-billion-weight-loss-industry/story?id=16297197.
3. http://www.cdc.gov/tobacco/data_statistics/fact_sheets/fast_facts/.
4. http://www.imshealth.com/deployedfiles/imshealth/Global/Content/Corporate/IMS%20Institute/RUOM-2013/IHII_Responsible_Use_Medicines_2013.pdf.
5. http://www.cms.gov/outreach-and-education/medicare-learning-network-mln/mlnproducts/downloads/chroniccaremanagement.pdf.
6. http://blogs.wsj.com/tech-europe/2013/06/03/wearable-tech-brings-health-benefits-but-may-exclude-many/.
7. http://www.forbes.com/sites/parmyolson/2014/06/19/wearable-tech-health-insurance/.
8. "Unleashing Government's 'Innovation Mojo': An Interview with the U.S. Chief Technology Officer," McKinsey & Company, June 2012, mckinsey.com/insights/public_sector/unleashing_governments_innovation_mojo.

9. apcdcouncil.org.

10. "The $2.7 Trillion Medical Bill," *New York Times*, June 1, 2013.

11. "Metrics for Transformation: Transparency," Health Care Incentives Improvement Institute, 2013.

12. http://www.catalyzepaymentreform.org/images/documents/2015_Report_PriceTransLaws_06.pdf.

13. "Transparency: The Most Powerful Driver of Health Care Improvement?" Health International, McKinsey & Company, 2011.

14. Ibid.

15. D. Love, W. Custer, and P. Miller, "All-Payer Claims Databases: State Initiatives to Improve Health Care Transparency, The Commonwealth Fund," September 2010, commonwealthfund.org/Publications/Issue- Briefs/2010/Sep/All-Payer-Claims-Databases.aspx#citation.

16. National Business Group on Health, https://www.businessgrouphealth.org/pressroom/pressRelease.cfm?ID=234.

17. "Transparency in the NHS Not Only Saves Lives—It Is a Fundamental Human Right," *The Guardian*, March 12, 2013.

18. "Transparency: The Most Powerful Driver of Health Care Improvement?" Health International, McKinsey & Company, 2011.

19. Ibid.

CHAPTER **7**

Implementation
Part 3

W e've talked about motivation, adherence, and choice, now—the first three consumer challenges we identified as our criteria. The next couple sort of blur together: coordination and effectiveness of care. How might we improve the coordination of care among healthcare providers, and how might we increase the effectiveness of healthcare services?

What we learned from the blueprint exercise was that consumers want time with their providers, and not to be "herded like cattle," as one interviewee said, and that doctors have information on them so that they don't feel like they're starting from scratch with each new doctor. Coordination and effectiveness are broad issues that mean various things and are large challenges to tackle. We could also argue that effectiveness would improve if coordination (and motivation, adherence, and choice) existed. But let's approach it in a more focused way.

Both coordination and the effectiveness of care could be enhanced by a lot of things we've already discussed: providers leveraging personal health clouds and self-generated data, using population health analytics to gain the 360-degree view, and using behavioral analytics to reach out more effectively to individuals. But the real issue is that patients are frustrated by the system—going from doctor to doctor without a single place for all their health information, having to fill out their history a hundred-and-one times, having very limited time with the provider, and much more. They're essentially noticing all the flaws of our data-sharing strategies and our volume-based system. Unfortunately, until policymakers and EHR companies figure out how to exchange data seamlessly and securely across multiple channels, consumers will have to deal with some of these frustrations. However, that's not the only way we can improve coordination and effectiveness, and luckily with changes emerging in the area of value-based care, there's a lot we can improve with the right tools to make the shift from volume to value a successful one.

WHY VOLUME TO VALUE?

Aside from the fact that the volume-based system creates dissatisfied consumers, another key factor in the shift is rising costs. Rising healthcare costs in the United States continue to be a critical issue and the fact that healthcare costs are unsustainably high and health outcomes are suboptimal raises concerns for all of us. Whether it's a provider trying to remain profitable while delivering the best patient care or a payer needing to manage services for new patient populations, the increasing costs and inadequate quality have affected everyone's financial and clinical decision making across the industry.

Healthcare decision makers and policymakers have attempted cost reduction and quality improvement techniques such as tackling fraud, waste, and abuse; reducing readmissions; and, most recently, extending coverage to millions of previously uninsured. While all of these small steps have typically generated positive change at different levels, they haven't created the systemic change necessary to drive value. In other words, achieving the best health outcomes per dollar spent hasn't materialized.

New incentives to create high value have begun to surface, such as accountable care and new reimbursements such as the Chronic Care Management Program. But while the recognition of value-based care has been established and embraced by some, how to achieve this ambiguous goal still remains a question. And rightly so—it's a big question. One on hand, providers want (and need) to remain profitable, payers have a business to run, and patients deserve the best care and don't want to be herded like cattle.

Addressing cost and quality effectively—often conflicting goals—is definitely a work in progress. And although some of the work requires a culture shift by organizations and individuals, a lot of it is going to rely on the right tools to enable consumer-centric, value-based care. So let's talk about some of the advanced analytics that can help healthcare organizations achieve this goal.

THE SHIFTING INCENTIVE AND ITS ADOPTION

For many consumers, it seems like providers are herding cattle because that's the way our system's structure has evolved. The healthcare system's performance incentives have historically been driven by the volume of services provided to patients and not the coordination of patient care, particularly when multiple providers are involved. As we talked about earlier, however, incentives are changing drastically, creating opportunities to gain a more consumer-centric focus on value. As commercial and government payers move away from a pay-for-volume system toward pay-for-value, financial risk is transferred to the provider(s) managing care. This changes incentives across the board for care and reimbursement, as providers now have to focus on better patient outcomes. It means that providers need to monitor the *total* path of care—for both cost and quality—and make necessary modifications such as treating patients holistically, reducing unwarranted admissions and readmissions, decreasing length of stays, improving cost-effective prescribing, and reducing variation in care. In other words, the implication for providers is achieving better patient outcomes using fewer resources.

The movement of transforming payment and delivery is still nascent but is moving rapidly. In fact, 75 percent of the providers that were surveyed in the 2013 Accountable Payment Survey expect to be engaged in a total cost of care (TCC) contract by 2017—a significant boost from the 35 percent that are currently under a TCC contract. Further, a March 2014 study by KPMG found that 44 percent of surveyed providers said they are "already working with bundled payments"—up from 38 percent in KPMG's October poll. Meanwhile, 20 percent said that they are not there yet but plan to be.[1]

Headway on the accountable care and shared-savings side has moved swiftly as well, despite mixed performance and results. The CMS Innovation Center's Pioneer ACO model, which launched in 2012, saw nine of 32 organizations exit the program after its first year, and nine of the remaining 23 organizations saved money, according to an independent audit.[2] Similarly, Medicare's Shared Savings Program has experienced uneven progress. Some of the 114 enrolled organizations have failed to reduce health spending while others—such as Heartland Regional Medical Center, which was in 2014 awarded $2.9 million for its success in accountable care[3]—have fared better. After two years of the program, CMS announced that the program saved Medicare about $385 million during this period, and that consumers reported more timely care and better communication with their providers, and that they're using inpatient hospital services less and have more follow-up visits from their providers after hospital discharge—all great news.

Last but not least, commercial payers and providers aren't the only ones moving forward with value-based care: State governments and Medicaid are getting on board, too, through CMS State Innovation Model grants. Arkansas, for example, is making waves nationally with its Medicaid bundled payment initiative.

■ ■ ■

Balancing both goals of cost reduction and quality improvement is complex, and while financial incentives for high value are critical, it's important to safeguard against inadvertent consequences. For example, reducing readmissions without understanding the complete view of a patient's care and needs is ineffective and doesn't consider the patient experience or patient outcomes. In general, cost reduction without regard to the outcomes achieved is dangerous and self-defeating, leading to false "savings" and potentially limiting effective care,[4] which leads to dissatisfied patients. That's why new payment and delivery models such as accountable care, patient-centered medical homes, bundled payments, and other shared-savings models require the right analysis tools to understand and measure value and outcomes.

While payers and providers are still investigating new methods for value-based care, perhaps the biggest challenge for these organizations, aside from cultural acceptance, is the lack of the right tools to understand patient data holistically. A 2014 survey by NAACOS found that learning to access and process data has been a significant challenge in ACOs achieving their goals. More specifically, ACOs have been challenged with finding suitable software and translating data into useful information for care managers and providers.[5] Fortunately, new methods and tools have emerged that can drive the success of these new models.

WHY EPISODE ANALYTICS?

All healthcare organizations, from standalone practices to integrated delivery networks, have historically struggled with understanding how all of the moving parts of patient care work together, which is critical if trying to create a seamless patient experience. So to help understand and analyze the care that's being delivered, healthcare organizations are adopting new tools like episode analytics.

Typically known as a bundle of care, clinical episodes define all of the services that could be provided around a significant number of health events and conditions. Episode analytics is a more advanced method of looking at clinical episodes and has distinct advantages over the traditional methods, because it focuses on quality alongside cost. New analytic innovations in episodes of care identify total cost of care at the individual patient level, provide flexibility to payers and providers in defining clinical episodes, enable providers to identify variations in care and opportunities for improvement, and allow organizations to assess and predict their financial risk and savings in value-based reimbursement agreements (Figure 7.1).

Some of this may sound complicated or foreign right now, but it'll get simpler as we continue. You'll find that if we use analytics, we'll be able to approach value-based care more comprehensively, addressing the needs of consumers, providers, and payers, and ultimately creating more effective and more coordinated care.

CONSTRUCTING AN EPISODE OF CARE

An episode of care is defined as a series of temporally contiguous healthcare services related to the treatment of a given spell of

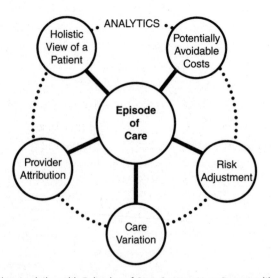

Figure 7.1 Using Analytics with Episodes of Care Creates New Opportunities for Innovation

illness or provided in response to a specific request by the patient or other relevant entity.[6] In simpler terms, it's a collection of care provided to treat a particular condition for a given length of time. Episodes of care are the foundation for any assessment of efficiency and are necessary in determining if a delivery system is achieving its intended purpose. This is because it analyzes care over time, rather than at a single point, and offers a better assessment of the patient's resultant health status.[7] Well-constructed episodes of care are instrumental to understanding and managing both cost and quality. They're also key to helping us understand the granularity of patient experiences.

WHAT CONSTITUTES AN EPISODE OF CARE?

Episode construction is a complex, multistep process in which many clinical rules must work together to identify what constitutes an episode. We're not going to talk about clinical rules and individual episodes, but let me tell you about how an episode is constructed.

The construction of an episode is initiated by a trigger event, such as an inpatient hospital admission or a diagnosis, which signals that a patient has a condition or procedure taking place. Then, using a patient's claims data, all of the claims that are relevant to a particular episode are grouped together. This grouping is done with clinical rules that identify a defined time period to capture all of the events related to the episode. You can use predefined definitions, like ones created by CMS, or you can create your own.

While each episode of care has unique rules for associating relevant events, there are some standards that exist. For example, chronic conditions, once triggered, don't terminate (because they're chronic). Procedures, like a knee replacement, are triggered by the procedure itself and have a lookback and look-forward period. And acute medical events, like a heart attack, start with the event (typically a hospitalization) and then look forward 30 days post-discharge.

Let's use the example of John Doe's knee replacement to illustrate episode construction. In the illustration in Figure 7.2, we see a trigger in John's claims that lets us know that a knee replacement episode has begun. Subsequently, all of the events related to the knee replacement are grouped together. Identifying which events are relevant

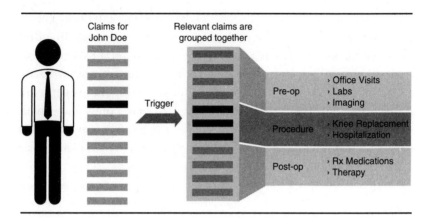

Figure 7.2 Constructing an Episode of Care with Claims Data

entails three time periods. First, there's the period leading up to the procedure, which can be referred to as the preoperative (pre-op) or lookback period. The lookback period for a knee replacement is 30 days, and for John's knee replacement this period may include events such as office visits, lab work, and some imaging. Then there's the procedure itself bounded by an inpatient or overnight stay. This includes the hospitalization and all professional services during the stay at the hospital. Finally, after John's discharged from the hospital, the postoperative (post-op) period begins, and it concludes when the patient has fully recovered and no longer needs treatment. For knee replacements, we look forward 90 days. In this stage of John's episode, there may be prescription medications, therapy, and more office visits.

CALCULATING THE COST OF AN EPISODE

The next step after we create the episode is to calculate the cost of it, by identifying which costs get allocated to the bundle. Costs are broken up into categories: typical, potentially avoidable, and unrelated. All of John's aforementioned events, such as the labs, office visits, and therapy, can be clinically categorized as typical costs—because they're typical in treating a knee replacement. Within the group of claims, though, there may also be claims for other (atypical) events that weren't actually relevant to his knee replacement. In other words, John may have had other services that weren't expected. For example, John has pain and swelling, goes to the emergency room, and gets admitted and treated for a wound infection. These events are unexpected, and, clinically, infections are considered preventable with good clinical practice and follow-up care. So these events are included in the total cost, but are differentiated as potentially avoidable costs (PACs) since they could've been prevented.

Finally, during the time period of John's knee replacement episode, other services may have occurred, such as a primary care visit for a cold. These services might be related to a different episode may be other services unrelated to this procedure. These costs don't get assigned to the cost of the knee replacement and are simply identified as "unrelated" costs.

PATIENT AND POPULATION: ANALYZING COSTS AND OUTCOMES

This method of constructing episodes and allocating costs lets us see the entirety of patient treatment as reflected in their claims data. Moreover, it provides an accurate measurement of total cost of care because costs measured at the condition or procedural level, not at the individual service level, is the most accurate way to measure them. And because value for the patient is created by providers' combined efforts over the full cycle of care, not just a single service, it structures patient data to allow us to track the entire experience of the patient. It's like a simpler version of an experience blueprint of a person's health condition/procedure.

Once episodes of care are created, we can analyze a variety of factors across a patient population and can create bundled payment models, measure the variation in care, and increase efficiencies among providers. For example, looking at the report in Figure 7.3, we can identify what clinical groups are represented in the patient population and how efficiently they're being treated.

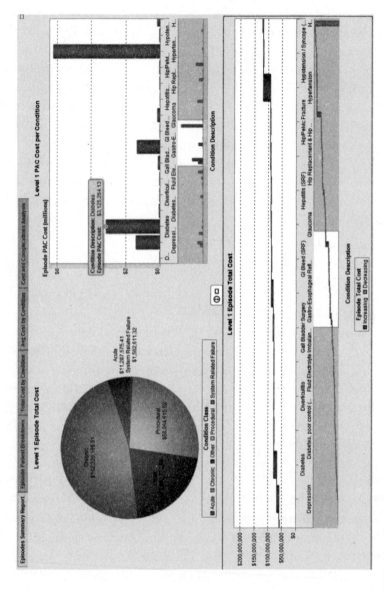

Figure 7.3 Episode Summary Report

This report shows the total cost of treating a variety of episodes across a population. The top-left pie-chart shows total cost divided into the five classes of episodes—acute, procedural, chronic, system-related failures, and other. Meanwhile, the other two graphs display the total cost of each episode across the population and the collective, potentially avoidable costs for each episode. Another view of the total cost of conditions can be seen in the next report (Figure 7.4), where the costs are grouped by Major Diagnostic Category (MDC). Imagine you're a large hospital system with multiple facilities. With this information you can quickly determine across all of your facilities what departments and conditions have room for improvement. The bars in the graph show the costs that are potentially avoidable and are areas for improvement. The little dots indicate the how much of the total costs are PACs; the higher the dot, the more the PACs. So let's say you want to look at your musculoskeletal system and connective tissue conditions; you see that the highest number of PACs lie within osteoarthritis. If you were in an interactive report, you could drill down into this condition and find out what services the PACs are coming from, and from what providers. Then, you could do a variety of things for improvement, like finding best practices from providers who have the least amount of PACs, and creating department-wide quality initiatives. In this case, you might approach pain medicine departments that treat osteoarthritis.

With the distinct visualizations we can easily see the episodes that contribute to the highest costs, as well those conditions that present the most potentially avoidable costs. In this particular example, it's evident that there are several million dollars of PACs in many of these episodes, with chronic conditions like diabetes and hypertension having some of the greatest amounts. Using this information, providers and payers can easily detect which patient populations are being treated and, based on the ratio of PAC to total cost, how efficiently they're being treated.

■ ■ ■

Going back to our osteoarthritis example, the next report (Figure 7.5) shows us the different services that are provided for osteoarthritic patients, how much they cost, including PACs, and how much variation there is for each service cost. At the bottom right, we can

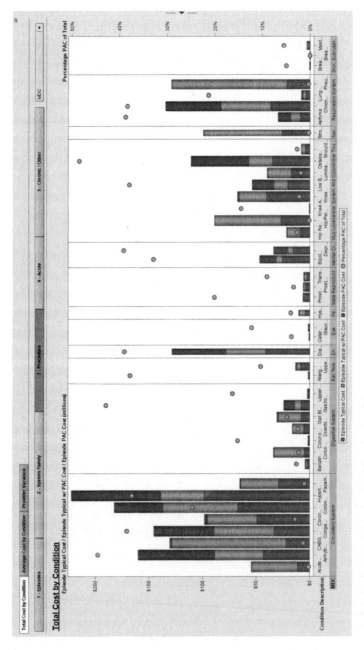

Figure 7.4 Episode Report Showing Total Cost by Condition

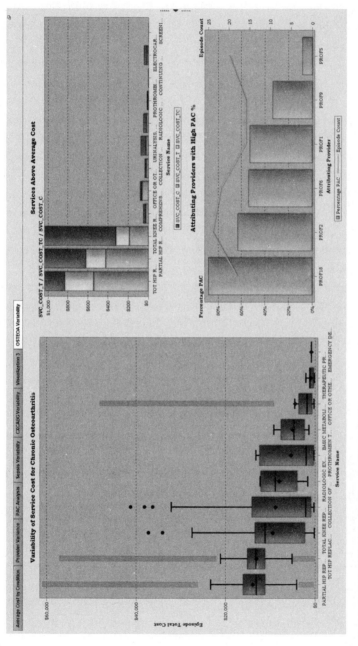

Figure 7.5 Details of Services for Chronic Osteoarthritis

also see the providers who have the highest PACs. This tells us exactly where to focus on bringing costs down. But more important, if PACs are high, it's likely that the quality of care and the patient experience are affected. It's a way to initiate improvements all around.

THE HOLISTIC VIEW OF A PATIENT

As you can imagine, a single patient may have many episodes taking place concurrently or in series. In fact this is common, and a reason that patients get frustrated when their providers aren't treating and coordinating all of their health issues collectively. For example, John may have a continuous diabetes episode in addition to his knee replacement. The previous reports show how we're treating individual episodes, but to analyze how we're treating individual patients, we need a holistic view of the patient, which is gained through associating episodes to each other based on distinct, clinical relationships.

A relationship between two episodes is called an *association*. In an association, two related conditions with overlapping episode time periods coexist, with one episode being subsidiary to the other. Associations are important because they allow us to see all of the services related to an individual's healthcare over a period of time.

PROVIDER PERFORMANCE

As discussed earlier, potentially avoidable costs (PACs) are those costs that were unexpected during an episode and can possibly be prevented. Because efficiency and effectiveness are key goals for new value-based models, reducing preventable events and costs are critical.

The report in Figure 7.6 shows an analysis of PACs for various procedures at the individual provider level, such as a knee replacement. If we analyzed these costs further at the individual claim line, we'd be able to learn the reasons behind these numbers, helping us to shape care coordination and cost containment efforts. Knowing what the main complications are among a group of providers can help shape both care coordination efforts and cost containment efforts.

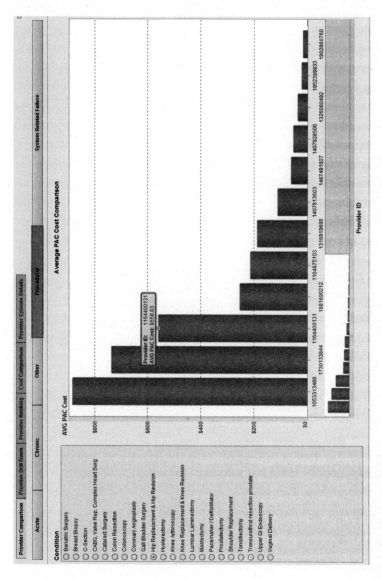

Figure 7.6 Provider Comparison Report

This also allows us to examine the performance of providers, which is another critical piece to value-based payment models, specifically bundled payments. In order for a provider to confidently participate in a bundled payment contract, it needs to have some level of confidence in its performance. Figure 7.6 is a useful report for analyzing performance. This report is similar to the osteoarthritis reports we looked at earlier, however, it compares providers against costs for procedures versus conditions—in this case knee replacement and knee revision.

Finally, in Figure 7.7 we can see the variation in both total cost and PACs and quickly identify the outliers. With this information, a payer or provider would be able to better decide on whom to contract with for bundled payments. Additionally, with accuracy in provider attribution, accountable care and patient-centered medical homes can easily recognize the owning or *conducting* providers of the episode.

■ ■ ■

Using episode analytics to enable value-based payment strategy, operations, and improvement is a big step forward for healthcare. It helps us address both cost and quality and lets us see the connection between the two. For patients, it means that providers will have a better, more complete approach to their health with a focus on achieving quality and improving the total experience. It also means that providers will have a means to coordinate with other providers, making new models like accountable care organizations more valuable and effective to consumers. While the road to value-based healthcare is a long one and is going to require the ideas and collaboration of lots of stakeholders, the right tools can help us gain the consumer-centric focus that we need. Episode is a critical piece to this transformation.

DIAGNOSIS AND PERSONALIZATION

Our final two criteria that we identified in Chapter 2 were diagnosis and personalization, and we saw both of these appear in Dennis's healthcare experience. Think back to his experience. Remember how it took several years for Dennis to get the right diagnosis for his condition?

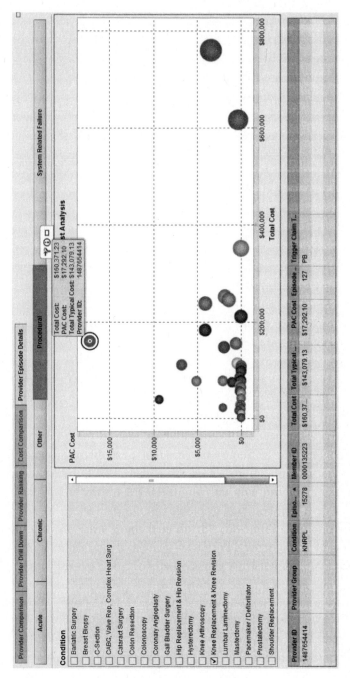

Figure 7.7 Provider Episode Details by Procedure

He spent time, money, and effort visiting multiple doctors, trying different medications, and basically going through a three-year roller-coaster ride to find out what was wrong with him. Unfortunately, this story isn't uncommon—whether it's a diagnosis that takes too long to make, a diagnosis that was never made, resulting in a worse condition or another condition, or even a prescribed medication that just wasn't the right fit for a person. As I've been discussing throughout the book, perhaps the whole goal of health analytics is that we get to a point where treatments are personalized for the individual. Every other industry is there, and healthcare, too, needs a higher level of personalization.

How might we increase the accuracy and timeliness of medical diagnostics and how might we create more personalization of care?

Enter machine learning. Machine learning has the potential to create that personalization by dramatically improving medical diagnostics and treatments. Recall that machine learning uses algorithms that iteratively learn from data and allow computers to find hidden insights without being programmed where to look. It learns from using more data, and what it provides is something called *artificial intelligence* (AI). It's basically smart computers creating smart answers. One of the driving forces in the machine learning and AI revolution is something called *deep learning algorithms*. This approach allows us to process information from nontraditional, unstructured sources like videos, images, and sounds. Deep learning algorithms are going to transform everything. Companies like Google and Facebook are already investing in this technology, and new inventions like real-time language translation and self-driving cars are already being created with machine learning. For example, using lots and lots of data on things like traffic-light patterns, speed limits, turns, distance from curbs, distance between cars, and more, the Google self-driving car is able to figure out what to do in different situations without a human. It's not a stretch to say that we'll soon be seeing self-driving cars on the road. And in healthcare, machine learning and artificial intelligence could be equally radical.

MACHINE LEARNING AND AI

We've talked about some of the applications of machine learning. For instance, automatically predicting health events and creating automated alerts and reminders for individuals are both applications of machine learning. One hospital in Dallas is already doing some of these things. They've actually been able to manage up to 70,000 children with asthma with just 70 resources using machine learning. By combining data about where patients live with environmental data from services such as weather.com and pollen.com, a cognitive system can spot correlations between the ragweed concentration in the air and asthma, and then send information or inhalers directly to children in areas where there's likely to be an uptick in asthma attacks. Without any human intervention, computers can provide individuals with accurate, usable information that could potentially save lives.

Soon, we'll see machine learning and AI become so much more groundbreaking in healthcare. Think about the billions (trillions, gazillions) of data points that could potentially be gathered with all of the data sources we've talked about—claims, EHRs, labs, imaging, mobile health, social media, and even genome data. Machine learning could be so powerful that it would find patterns in all of this unimaginable data, and by using an individual's genomic structure, tell us what treatment would work best for that person. For example, two women, both with the same type of lung cancer, may have entirely different treatment needs. One may be an active athlete while the other is overweight and leads a sedentary life. One may be diabetic while the other has no chronic conditions. One may be in her late fifties while the other just turned 40. All of these differences could mean different treatments, but finding treatments for specific types of people at such a granular level is nearly impossible for doctors and scientists. Critical information is lost in the mountains of data and it would take years to sort through all of the data to find the correlations and clues between all of these data points. As big data gets bigger and bigger in healthcare, it'll only become more of a challenge, becoming humanly impossible to use this data effectively.

That's why machine learning is so exciting for diagnosing and treating conditions. Eric Xing, a professor in the machine learning department at Carnegie Mellon, explains, "Every patient is different. You can take a very simplistic view. Say, breast cancer should be treated by drug A or B. But uniqueness in lifestyle, environment, and other health factors makes someone a unique individual. AI might take information from not just one doctor but many doctors' experiences and it can pull out information from different patients that share similarities." Scientists at Carnegie Mellon University and the University of Pittsburgh are already working on using artificial intelligence to filter through electronic health records, diagnostic imaging, prescriptions, genomic profiles, insurance records, and even data from wearable devices, to create healthcare plans designed not just for a specific disease but for specific types of people. The researchers are hoping to be able to create designer treatments, head off epidemics, and find cures to deadly diseases.

■ ■ ■

Machine learning could be the Holy Grail in curing some of the most deadly diseases. Eric Topol, author of the book *The Patient Will See You Now* (Basic Books), thinks that we're in for some radical improvements in preventing conditions and diseases that have attack characteristics like heart attacks, strokes, seizures, asthma, and autoimmune diseases. He says that using *omic* (genome, proteome, or metabolome) tools like DNA sequencing or RNA tags, we'll be able to identify individuals at high risk for certain diseases. Also, wearable or embedded biosensors could be used to continuously monitor individuals well before signs, tissue destruction, or a clinical crisis develops. This will involve contextual computing and deep/machine learning. Topol believes that in the years ahead it should be feasible and increasingly practical to track large cohorts of people with conditions of interest. And as a result of tracking these large cohorts, that one or more of these conditions will actually become preventable in the next 20 years.

Preventing heart attacks and strokes sounds preposterous in some ways: it's predictive analytics on a whole new, unimaginable level, giving us so much precision of information that it seems a little unreal. But it is in fact real, and it's coming.

NATURAL LANGUAGE PROCESSING

In the next decade we could even see our phones or other gadgets diagnosing our conditions for us. With natural language processing (NLP), which uses machine learning to understand human speech, we could see services like a Siri for healthcare, using machine learning to translate everyday words into diagnoses. Imagine what this could do for the accessibility to healthcare. Companies like Skype, are in fact, already experimenting with real-time language translations; advancements like these could potentially diminish language barriers to care.

One day, NPL could become so accurate that it could capture individual sentiments as well. Actually, NPL is already so advanced that it can capture subtleties, nuances, and idioms in our language. What if, instead of waiting for your doctor's appointment, you told your phone the details of how you're feeling, and it took that information, along with all the other data from your personal health cloud, to provide you a diagnosis and treatment plan all in a matter of seconds? Or what if you voiced your health goals to a device and it knew you so well that it gave you the perfect combination of nudges and alerts to meet your target? What do you think all of this would do to the role of the physician? What do you think it would do to the role of the consumer? Nobody really knows, but one thing's for sure—machine learning will have a dramatic role in healthcare.

■ ■ ■

While some of this seems farfetched, it's actually closer to us than it seems and people are already working on these advancements. One start-up company, Enlitic, is focusing on making medical diagnostics faster, more accurate, and more accessible. They're creating tools for providers to leverage deep learning methods that would allow physicians to use the vast amount of data, like medical images (x-rays, MRIs, CT scans, 3D medical images), doctors' notes, and structured lab tests, to help them diagnose patients. Jeremy Howard, CEO and founder of Enlitic, believes that medical diagnosis at its heart is a data problem, and that turning all of this data into a diagnosis and a proposed intervention is the biggest opportunity for positive impact using data that he's seen in his 20+ years in the data science field.

Another company, Lumiata, is doing similar and equally inventive work with something called graph analysis, through which it can connect all the pieces of data that physicians see about patients on a daily basis, along with all the knowledge that they've acquired over the years. It's a big data system that's gathered more than 160 million data points from textbooks, journal articles, public datasets, and other places in order to build graph representations of how illnesses and patients are connected. The technical term for what Lumiata does is *multidimensional probability distribution*, but as Ash Damle, CEO of the company, explains, it basically boils down to understanding how time, location, and behavior come together to affect how a disease develops and progresses. The technology analyzes graphs containing tens of thousands of nodes (e.g., symptoms, diseases, and patient data points) and weighted edges (e.g., the connections between them all and how strong they are) in well under a second. That's *one* second. That means it can be used for real-time care, making analytics at the point-of-care possible for medical providers.

Damle gives the example of symptoms such as pneumonia and confusion to explain Lumiata. He says these symptoms are fairly common in younger patients and older patients, but not really for patients in between those ages. A graph analysis might help a nurse or a doctor find something abnormal within these age groups in between, and then instruct him or her on potential follow-up questions. Because various weak signals build up over time, it's important to see what may have been missed because all the little things could amount to something significant.

■ ■ ■

Enlitic and Lumiata are definitely doing some neat things with machine learning and AI, and there's still so much more to be done. My colleague, Dr. Mark Wolff, often talks about using these same tools to gain even more details of diagnoses, which consider things like the levels of severity. For example, if a patient is diagnosed with a certain condition, what's the severity of his or her condition? And how does the severity impact the treatment? We don't always know how severity correlates to various treatments, and having this type of information would let us make choices on medications and treatment plans, allowing us to understand if an individual is right for a certain drug, for instance. Subsequently, it'd also help with pharmaceutical and clinical research in developing drugs that are suitable for certain levels of severity of particular conditions. This impact could be huge, as so many millions of people are taking medications each day that aren't helping them.

In fact, the top-10 highest-grossing drugs in the United States help only between 1 in 25 and 1 in 4 of the people who take them. For some drugs, such as statins, as few as one out of 50 people may benefit. There are even drugs that are harmful to certain ethnic groups because of the bias toward white Western participants in classical clinical trials. That's why President Obama announced a national Precision Medicine Initiative in 2015 that focuses on using the variability in genes, environment, and lifestyle for each person to create more effective and personalized drugs and treatments. Tools like machine learning and AI are going to be instrumental in implementing precision medicine and in making genetic diagnoses possible through learning about new disease genes. Not only will they allow us to find very personalized treatments and interventions, but they'll also help the system to reduce its spend on both drug development and prescription drugs.

■ ■ ■

Even though the concept of machine learning isn't new, the growth in the areas of machine learning and artificial intelligence is really just beginning to take shape in healthcare. It's definitely one of the areas that excites me the most and one that I think is going to be a game changer for our industry.

NOTES

1. NASDAQ OMX GlobeNewswire, "More Healthcare Providers Using Bundled Payment Systems, But Some Still Undecided Ahead of CMS Application Deadline: KPMG Survey," April 15, 2014.
2. Melanie Evans, "Providers Net Uneven Results from ACO Experiment," *Modern Healthcare*, January 30, 2014.
3. Christine Kern, "ACO Success Stories," *Health IT Outcomes*, April 10, 2014.
4. Michael E. Porter, "What Is Value in Health Care?" *New England Journal of Medicine*, December 23, 2010.
5. National Association of ACOs, "National ACO Survey Conducted November 2013," January 21, 2014.
6. M. C. Hornbrook, A. V. Hurtado, and R. E. Johnson, "Health Care Episodes: Definition, Measurement and Use," *Medical Care Review*, 1985, 42(2): 163–218.
7. National Quality Forum: Patient-Focused Episodes of Care: "Measurement Framework: Evaluating Efficiency across Patient-Focused Episodes of Care," 2010.

CHAPTER **8**

Innovation

PUTTING IT ALL TOGETHER

You may be overwhelmed by all the analytics-speak I've bombarded you with. If you are, I don't blame you. We've covered a lot of potential solutions to create a more consumer-centric healthcare system. Let's reflect back on all the ideas we've discussed.

We started by discovering issues within the system through the eyes of the consumers: What are their experiences like? What are their thoughts of the system? By connecting with them through their experiences, we were able to gain *empathy* for them as the end-users. The experience blueprint helped us to better understand patient experiences across the entire continuum of care, including their needs, feelings, and thoughts at each step of the way. This insight helped us to define our *criteria*.

Once we identified our criteria, we searched for *inspiration* to address these challenges. We looked at multiple other industries such as banking, retail, and e-commerce that have solved these similar problems, and gleaned insight on how they were able to do it. This inspired us to expand our thinking into a new type of healthcare system. Resultantly, in the *ideation* stage, we created ideas for a new system, one in which the consumer is empowered and engaged in achieving optimal health.

Finally, in the *implementation* stage, we figured out how we could reach this ideal healthcare system, combining *desirability* with *feasibility* and *viability* as we approached new solutions that ultimately address our criteria and our consumer needs and wants. See Figure 8.1 for what we came up with.

Motivation	>	Population Health
Adherence		Behavioral Analytics
		Behavior Change Platforms
Choice	>	Data Transparency
		All-Payer Claims Databases
		Personalized Health Plans
Coordination	>	Episode Analytics
Effectiveness		Potentially Avoidable Costs
		Holistic View of Patient
Diagnosis	>	Machine Learning
Personalization		Artificial Intelligence
		Natural Language Processing

Figure 8.1 Solutions We Identified to Address our Criteria

- To address the lack of motivation and patient adherence, we identified population health analytics, behavioral analytics, and behavior change platforms that can help us to understand consumers better, create recommendation engines, and provide personalized guidance for consumers.

- To create consumer choice throughout the system, we discussed the importance of data transparency and a state-government initiative—the all-payer claims database, which can inform consumers on price and quality while they shop for healthcare.

- Coordination and effectiveness of care, we learned, can be improved by analyzing the *total* path of care, using episode analytics to understand how cost and quality are interconnected, and how treating patients can be done more holistically.

- Finally, we talked about machine learning, artificial intelligence, and natural language processing to make medical diagnostics and personalization of care a reality.

DESIGN THINKING TOOLS

By taking you through this process, my intent was to emphasize the philosophy that we should start with the consumer, identify a vision for a new way of doing something, and *then* think about how technology may fit in to create value. Generating a deep understanding of consumer needs and desires first is the foundational component to a human-centered approach to problem solving.

Design thinking lets us start with people and focus on their needs to innovate at the intersection of business, technology, and people. The process can lead to radical, experience innovation, which is why it's such a great tool for taking healthcare into the experience and transformation economy. I used design thinking to structure my thought processes for this book and to give you ideas for how to create a more human-centered approach to healthcare. However, there are many other key elements to design thinking that are beyond what I can apply in a book.

Perhaps one of the signature aspects of design thinking is that it's an iterative approach. During the life cycle of the project, teams can iterate by cycling through the process multiple times and also by iterating within a single step. This ensures that our end-users stay involved throughout the process, and lets us be agile in creating and implementing new ideas.

Prototyping is another essential for design thinking and is done early and often to test ideas with users during the innovation process. Creating prototypes and testing them to receive user feedback helps us to continuously refine products and services to ultimately make something that consumers will love. Prototyping is critical because understanding human interaction is key to generating the best possible solution.

When we created Remedy, we created a prototype very rapidly and got it into the hands of providers and patients to see how they interacted with it. Then, through focus groups and interviews, we identified what they liked about it and what they didn't like about it. We kept iterating through this process and through multiple prototypes, making refinements as we received feedback. At some points we even had to go back to the discovery stage to ensure that we had defined our problem correctly, or to define it at a more granular level. We iterated until we nailed down exactly what the end-users wanted and what met both their functional and emotional needs, ultimately creating something that they love.

In the case of health analytics it's important that we use agile technologies that let us iterate and test new concepts quickly. The sooner we can get new concepts into the hands of users, receive feedback, and understand their value impact on consumers, the faster we can make progress toward experience innovation. That's why tools like Hadoop, cloud analytics, and visual analytics are so important for innovating in healthcare.

Regardless of the challenge you're addressing, whether a system-level issue or a granular issue, using human-centered design principles to create healthcare solutions can focus your efforts on end-users, helping us all advance toward a more consumer-centric healthcare system. The process I presented here is one suggestion of a framework, but ultimately, you'll make the process your own and adapt it to the style, work, and goals of your organization. My hope is that you consider human-centered design principles as you work on creating transformative healthcare solutions.

EXPONENTIAL GROWTH

In 2013, I got an opportunity to see Dr. Peter Diamandis speak at SAS's annual Healthcare and Life Sciences Executive Conference and he blew me away with his discussion on linear versus exponential thinking. He believes that while technologies are growing exponentially, humans are carrying on with linear and local thinking, creating a gap between what society *believes* to be possible and what technology is *actually* making possible. As an example, he said to consider where you'll be if you take 30 linear steps in any direction; that's easy, right? Now, try imagining how far you'd get with 30 exponential steps (2^{30}). Most of us wouldn't realize that this would allow you to circumambulate the world 26 times!

Diamandis utilizes a framework of six Ds to think about exponential growth processes in technology. While we've talked about multiple technologies, some further along than others, I think it's relevant to use a wider perspective and apply these six Ds to the healthcare industry at large.

1. *Digitized:* According to Diamandis, anything that becomes digitized goes through exponential growth, and there's no doubt that this one is huge in healthcare. In fact, the digital health field is expected to *triple* by 2018, with the mobile health (mHealth) market leading the way; mHealth is predicted to expand at a compound annual growth rate (CAGR) of 47.6 percent from 2015 to 2020.[1] Digitization opens the doors for analytics, and with this radical growth it's indisputable that digital health will help take us toward our vision of personal health clouds. Further, with more than 80 percent of U.S. doctors today having utilized an EHR system in their practice, as compared to 57 percent in 2011, we're in for the most widespread digitization than in possibly any other industry.

2. *Deceptive:* Diamandis says that early stages of exponential growth processes may be deceptively linear. He often gives the example of 3D printing, saying that it's been around for 30 years but that we're only hearing about it in recent years because the early years of its development were very slow. I think the same could be said about health analytics. We've

been analyzing healthcare data for decades. However, the way we analyzed it hasn't changed until now. The same can be said about various types of health data. Claims data, for example, isn't new, but the possibilities for it have just recently begun to be explored. Although we're beginning to see some organizations revamp their health data strategies, many are still operating with incremental steps of progress, which is making the gap between their linear and exponential thinking wider and wider. One thing's for sure—organizations will have no choice but to exploit new analytics technologies if they want to stay relevant in the industry.

3. *Disruption:* "A disruptive technology is any innovation that creates a new market and disrupts an existing one," says Diamandis. Between the explosion of big data, digital health, and the IoT, health analytics is creating a plethora of new markets. New ways to use health data and to apply analytics are surfacing across every corner of healthcare, whether it's through mobile devices and wearables, leveraging deep machine learning, or creating behavior change platforms. In fact, the funding of digital health start-ups is expected to double over the next three years and reach 6.7 billion by 2017.[2] Plus, healthcare IT jobs are sweeping the industry, with newly created roles like chief mobile healthcare officers and digital health strategists. Astoundingly, the hospital sector gained more than 100,000 jobs in only a year's time[3] and I'm certain that the radical transformations in healthcare are triggering this surge.

4. *Dematerialized:* Dematerialization means that several technologies *dematerialize* into one small technology. For example, a TV, flashlight, camera, and alarm clock can now all be found on your smartphone; no longer do you have to buy four individual devices. Healthcare analytics technologies are already beginning to dematerialize. With tools like Hadoop and cloud analytics, we're finding that we can do everything including store data, process and cleanse data, and analyze data in one powerful environment. Gone are the days of costly data servers that simply stored data. Now, we have remarkably low-cost and

scalable alternatives that let us do basically whatever we want with our data.

5. *Demonetized:* As we just discussed, new, dematerialized technologies are offering less expensive methods for health analytics. Affordable commodity hardware is now available for big data, and with emerging software-as-a-service models for health analytics, users don't even need additional hardware; they can analyze their data simply by logging in through the Web.

6. *Democratized:* Democratization is the spread of technology across the world, and for health analytics, democratization is a big deal. There will be 3 billion more people on the Internet by 2020, giving people a voice in the global discourse for the first time. While that's impactful across all industries, in healthcare it means that we'll start seeing and hearing things about where and what types of healthcare conditions exist and the perceived quality and satisfaction of healthcare experiences. Also, as data transparency initiatives become more widespread, the channels for health analytics will grow exponentially, opening up data to new users for research and innovation.

I think all the signs are headed toward grand exponential growth in healthcare. The inevitable disruption of the healthcare industry is going to make for some exciting times in health analytics. What do you think will be some of the biggest disruptors in healthcare?

■ ■ ■

All of this discussion around healthcare innovation reminds me of the health analytics framework that I talked about earlier. We have so many issues to address in healthcare, and so many new tools and technologies available to us, not to mention the huge wave of healthcare reform taking shape. By leveraging the dematerialization and demonetization of new analytics tools, we're going to be able to, for the first time, create the visionary health clouds that we discussed in the ideation chapter. Bringing tools and tech together with real consumer issues is going to make these health clouds so powerful that they'll incorporate all of the capabilities we talked about into a single space. That means interoperability and integration like we've never imagined. And it means that whether you're a payer, a provider, or a consumer, you're going to be either creating or receiving more seamless healthcare experiences that are made possible through big data analytics. Our health analytics framework may actually end up looking more like Figure 8.2.

■ ■ ■

In order to create the seamless experiences that we need throughout the healthcare system, we need solutions to work together just like what's depicted in the new framework. All the solutions we identified throughout the implementation stage—including population health analytics, behavioral analytics, behavior change platforms, data transparency, episode analytics, holistic view of consumers, deep learning, and AI—while powerful on their own, are even more powerful in tandem. Because each one helps us at different stages of the healthcare experience, together they can assemble all the pieces to create the seamless, integrated experience that we're striving for. From a feasibility standpoint, all of the solutions we've identified can be made possible with the same data sources, and can all be supported with tools like Hadoop and cloud analytics. From a viability perspective, these strides in analytics are going to help healthcare organizations to make the necessary changes to succeed in our new value-based health economy.

If I had to take this thought process a step further, I'd say that all of it can be summed up with one word: *modernization* (Figure 8.3).

MODERNIZATION

Modernization is a vague word that means different things depending on the context, but by Oxford's definition, it's the *process of adapting to modern needs or habits, typically by installing modern equipment or adopting modern ideas or methods*. Let's break down that definition as it relates to healthcare.

Adapting to Modern Needs or Habits

In today's world, our modern need is for fast-and-easy things. People expect immediate access to other people and to information. Whether it's interacting with a technology or waiting in line, there's a

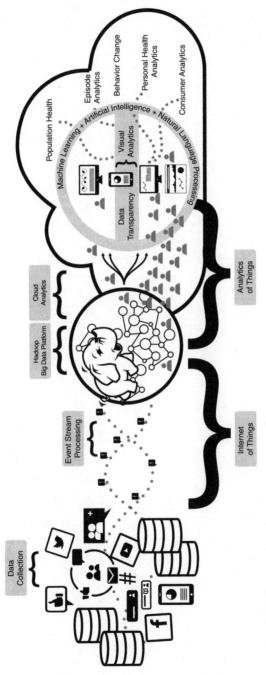

Figure 8.2 New Health Analytics Framework

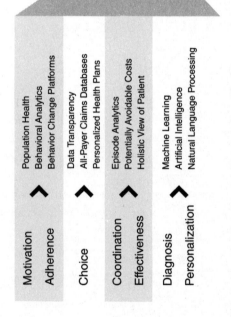

Figure 8.3 Everything can be Summed Up into *modernization*

common theme of increasing immediacy in today's modern culture. In healthcare, this type of instant access isn't a simple thing to achieve.

Taking that notion of today's world, and by learning from healthcare consumers, we can create a new lens through which to see healthcare. This lens is what we need to adapt to the modern-day consumer's needs and habits. Considering consumer desires, their environment, lifestyle, and the way they engage with other services in the experience economy will help us create a new health economy that integrates into our daily lives.

Adopting Modern Ideas or Methods

Modern ideas and methods could refer to a variety of things, but there are a few that come to mind. When I think of modern ideas in healthcare, I think of novel data analytics strategies, data-driven decision making, as well as new methods of payment or delivery in healthcare. I also think it's applicable to new ways of thinking about innovation and problem solving, like design thinking and the six Ds of exponential growth. What's most important is that a shift in mindset occurs within healthcare systems to embrace new ideas and methods that can help us to innovate rapidly.

Installing Modern Equipment

We've talked about modern equipment a lot throughout the book, and to me, this piece is all about your technology infrastructure. Do you have the right platforms in place to create optimal value to consumers? Do you have access to the right data? Are you able to handle large amounts of data? Are you using your data to its potential? It's also about adapting to new consumer technologies, whether it's a smartphone, a wearable device, or integrating into the Internet of Things.

■ ■ ■

Healthcare modernization efforts certainly won't take place overnight, and the cultural and technology shifts that must take place for modernization are sizable. Although bringing modern ideas, methods, and equipment to meet modern needs and habits of healthcare consumers will take time, new approaches such as human-centered design and new technologies like big data analytics will make the entry paths quicker and easier.

TRADITIONAL → MODERN

When we think about the different aspects of modernization—methods, equipment, ideas—most of us probably immediately think of the barriers to modernization. In healthcare, we face cultural, technological, and regulatory barriers greater than other industries, which often inhibit us from system-wide innovation. How do we ensure that the downstream path from our consumer issues is met with modernization of methods, ideas, and equipment?

The answer is interoperability. For solutions to work together, for the data to work together, for the *system* to work together, we need interoperability. In fact, under the definition of a system, which is *a set of connected things or parts forming a complex whole*, it's farfetched to say that healthcare is actually a system. Frankly stated, things just don't work together as they should.

To create interoperability, EHRs can be our best friends if they don't become our worst enemies before that. While it's great news that the adoption of EHRs is rapidly growing, we're now facing the challenge of countless types of EHRs, with insufficient standardization, that don't communicate with each other. *Health information exchanges* have been attempting to solve these issues for some time, and while the nation has made dramatic advancements in the digitization and sharing of health information, we've still got a long way to go. To put that into perspective, think about the last few times you've had a doctor's appointment. Chances are that for the majority of times you still have to provide your own medical history and information to each new doctor. The reason that still happens is because although we've made a massive shift from paper records to electronic records, both provider-to-provider and provider-to-consumer data sharing have encountered many roadblocks. Actually, only 14 percent of office-based providers electronically share patient information with other providers today, and only half of U.S. hospitals can search for critical health information from outside sources, such as an ER visit or an office visit.[4] Even with the proliferation of health information exchanges, seamless data sharing is very nascent in our industry.

I talked about health information exchanges and interoperability a little in the first chapter; to cover it in depth would make for a book in itself given the momentum and activities over the last decade. While the industry has only scratched the surface of interoperability, there has been notable progress made. First, almost 80 percent of office-based physicians now use an EHR system to collect patient data. This is great news for the path to interoperability. With every health record that becomes digitized and every provider we get to securely share data, we'll take a step closer to improving healthcare experiences. The other good news is that all 50 states now have some form of health information exchange services available to support care. That means that there's existing infrastructure we can leverage and build upon for the sharing and analysis of data.

On the not-so-positive side, there are many lingering barriers that are limiting us from full-on interoperability. For instance, most states have different laws and regulations for sharing health information across state lines. That makes it virtually impossible to take your health data with you across multiple states. Also, as I've previously mentioned, health information isn't sufficiently standardized. This makes it difficult to link records and to collect a full picture of an individual's healthcare. Last, but not least, there are trust barriers that need to be overcome in order for people to feel comfortable and secure in their data being shared. Trust is encapsulated by a larger privacy and security barrier, the importance of which I can't emphasize enough. Healthcare data security has to be significantly enhanced. Given recent incidents of data breaches with large enterprises such as Anthem and Premera, it's becoming increasingly important to maintain the security of personal data.

INTEROPERABILITY ROADMAP

What's the plan for interoperability? A lot of us in the industry are working toward taking down the barriers and getting interoperability to where it needs to be. In fact, the ONC's ten-year Interoperability Roadmap—the federal government's bold vision for interoperability—while challenging, has the potential to bring new types of connectivity to healthcare that will improve care and reduce costs. There are three big milestones in the roadmap that are particularly noteworthy. First, by the end of 2017, the majority of individuals and providers will be able to send, receive, find, and use a common set of clinical information. Second, by the end of 2020, the goal is to expand the connectivity to mobile health and wearables, getting insight on those 80 percent of factors outside of the healthcare system that impact health. The third and final goal is to create, by the end of 2024, a *learning health system* that promotes continuous learning and improvement through the analysis of all types of data.

I'm eager to see how the vision of interoperability unfolds and excited to be a part of the transformations. Without connectivity throughout the system and a simple way to exchange healthcare information between providers and consumers, our ability to modernize healthcare and make it a human-centered system is impossible. Getting things to talk to each other is definitely the biggest hurdle we need to cross in the industry. We're seeing this issue not only with electronic health records, but with every other type of health data, and especially self-generated data. One company, Validic, is already addressing this issue aggressively. Validic is a Durham, NC–based company that's addressing what they refer to as the "Digital Health Divide"— a lack of access by physicians and other healthcare professionals to patient-recorded data. Drew Schiller, CTO of the company, says, "The data must be accessible by healthcare professionals to make a difference."[5] To diminish the divide, they've built a digital health platform that lets healthcare organizations connect to mobile health apps, wearables, and medical devices and sensors through one simple connection. It's completely agnostic to devices and platforms, which makes it possible to continuously connect to all varieties of devices and applications as they come to market. It's exactly what we need to create a continuous stream of interoperability that'll simplify access to health data.

Imagine if we had these types of single connectors for all of our health data—be it claims, EHRs, or other types of data. All of a sudden the idea of establishing health clouds doesn't seem as intimidating or farfetched anymore.

NOTES

1. http://mhealthintelligence.com/news/mobile-health-market-digital-healthcare-technology-expands.
2. https://www.accenture.com/us-en/insight-healthcare-it-start-up-funding-fueling-digital-disruption.aspx.
3. http://www.forbes.com/sites/dandiamond/2015/06/05/hospitals-jobs-growth-is-suddenly-booming/.
4. http://healthit.gov/sites/default/files/shared_nationwide_interoperability_roadmap.pdf.
5. http://validic.com/wp-content/uploads/2015/04/Validic-Bridges-Interoperability-Gap.pdf.

CHAPTER **9**

Individual

Well, you made it to the last chapter of the book and through the patchwork of discussion on big data, analytics, and the design thinking process. Here are the different areas we've covered.

- *Insight:* We started in Chapter 2 with gaining insight, learning from consumers themselves about what they think and feel about our healthcare system. We learned about their experiences, and by creating an experience blueprint we were able to understand many different challenges at various touchpoints of the system that a person may encounter. This helped us to define our criteria.

- *Inspiration:* Once we identified our criteria, our search for inspiration to address these challenges began. We found that industries such as banking, retail, and e-commerce have solved similar problems and we discussed how they've done it through the use of data.

- *Ideation:* In the ideation chapter, we imagined a new type of healthcare system, one in which the consumer is empowered and engaged in achieving optimal health. New ideas, like personal health clouds, were introduced.

- *Implementation:* We went through three chapters on implementation, starting with the tools available to us and how we can utilize them to address our criteria. Then we delved into many different health analytics tools that can help us to craft better healthcare experiences.

- *Innovation:* The innovation chapter shed light on exponential growth and modernization of healthcare. We identified that interoperability is a foundation for modernization efforts.

■ ■ ■

This brings us to our final chapter. I named this chapter "Individual" because that's what the entire book is about: improving health for each individual. We identified early on that passive consumption is no longer an option in today's experience economy. Individuals must be active participators in their healthcare, and healthcare experiences must be reinvented to be seamlessly integrated into our daily lives. Creating better experiences for individuals through things like coordination, more effective care, and personalization can lead to better health outcomes and reduced costs. Further, better experiences that integrate people into the system as active consumers will help each individual to achieve better health.

We've learned that we can design an entirely new healthcare system in which individuals drive their own health journeys. Moreover, we learned that the patient of healthcare is no longer merely a patient. Creating a system that focuses on wellness in addition to sickness and that's driven by the individual results in the patient taking on a new role as a *consumer*. That's the patient revolution that's unfolding.

As the patient takes on a new role, this shift demands a huge transformation of the healthcare ecosystem, one of ultimate connectivity and modernization. These are big challenges to address, but I'm certain that we're getting there. With the availability of new tools and technologies that let us establish simplified, modern data systems, we can appropriately support initiatives in healthcare innovation that are focused on value for the consumer.

New flexible and scalable healthcare IT systems will support more efficient and effective care, scientific advancements in medicine, and a continuously improving health system that empowers individuals, customizes treatment, and accelerates cures of deadly diseases. Additionally, the new health IT ecosystem will also support health outside of the confines of the care system, engraining health into daily behaviors and lifestyles.

WHERE DO WE GO FROM HERE?

It's exciting to think about how the patient revolution is bringing so many new ways to align healthcare incentives with consumer needs and increase innovation exponentially throughout our system. The big challenge is of course crossing the barriers we talked about and building this new ecosystem. Fortunately, we're seeing the walls of interoperability beginning to come down, legacy IT systems being replaced with modern ones, and new products, solutions, and policies being created that are bringing more consumer-centricity. Where do we go from here and how do we continue to make progress?

Tim Brown's thoughts on experience innovation helped me to start thinking about our logical next steps. In his book *Change by Design* (Harper Collins), Brown says that the best and most successful experience brands have many things in common that can provide us with some guidelines. These guidelines resonated with me as I thought about closing remarks for this book, because although we aren't developing a healthcare "brand," we are seeking to create successful experiences. I think that these guidelines hold true across any type of systemic, product, or service innovation in today's experience economy:

- A successful experience requires active consumer participation.

We've talked about the topic of active participation extensively throughout the book. Active participation in the healthcare system can create a new landscape for the industry, with strengthened consumer–provider relationships, team-based approaches to health, and more accountability for health outcomes across all stakeholders. A system that creates active participators will naturally bring empowerment, engagement, and a path to improved health while increasing consumer satisfaction with the system.

In essence, everything we discussed in this book was about creating active participation, either directly or indirectly. As we found through Dennis's experience, keeping individuals engaged and motivated can be difficult, and we talked about Fogg's Behavior = Motivation+Ability+Trigger (B=MAT) behavior model and using data analytics to create new behaviors that integrate into existing behaviors and lifestyles. We also talked about using data analytics to identify how best to reach out to individuals. Other types of analytics applications, like population health and episode analytics, create personalization of the total path of care and ultimately more effective care and happier consumers. What's often referred to as "patient engagement" in the industry is a core component that hasn't been addressed as effectively as it should be; the new health economy is changing this dramatically, though, allowing us to create a system that encourages active participation.

- A customer experience that feels authentic, genuine, and compelling is likely to be delivered by employees operating within an experience culture themselves.

I think that there are two parts to this one that make it very relevant to the healthcare system. The first part is a customer experience that feels authentic, genuine, and compelling. It's important that as we create a more connected, digitized, and data-driven system we don't lose sight of what's most important to healthcare: the human element. If done right, the use of big data and analytics can create a more authentic, genuine, and compelling experience, but it can also create more frustrations and disruptions in workflow if not crafted appropriately. That's why design thinking can be a toolkit for change to tackle system-wide challenges we face in healthcare. At the end of the day, technology will help support better care and better health, but ultimately healthcare boils down to human interactions; that's what design thinking takes us back to.

The second part of the statement is about employees operating within an experience culture themselves. Most of what we've talked about has been focused on the consumer impact of new innovations. However, our front-line workers in medicine, the healthcare providers, will increasingly become the end-users of many of these new solutions. Their adoption of new tools and technologies is a driving factor for change, and their support is critical. Unfortunately, the medical school curriculum hasn't been modified to address these emerging needs, which is something that's inevitable for success. Wyatt Decker, chief executive of the Mayo Clinic's operations in Arizona, acknowledged this gap and hit the nail on the head when he recently said that "the reality is that most medical schools are teaching the same way they did one hundred years ago." In fact, the core structure of medical school has been in place since 1910 and critics have for long faulted U.S. medical education for being hidebound, imperious, and out of touch with modern healthcare needs.[1] Decker thinks that it's time to blow up the current model and start focusing on the science of healthcare delivery—things like how to focus on prevention and wellness and how to work in a team. In order to meet the demands of the nation's changing healthcare system, he says we must ask ourselves, "How do we want to train tomorrow's doctors?"[2]

With the system rapidly becoming data-driven, value-based, and consumer-centric, doctors must be prepared to meet the demands of the new health economy. As more and more data becomes available on patients, on populations, and on treatments, and data becomes an essential tool for providers, new skills in utilizing this information will be critical. For example, with advancements in machine learning and data streaming it may be less necessary to memorize facts, as they may quickly become irrelevant as new knowledge becomes generated in real-time. What will be important is to understand how to use new information and analytics for better, more coordinated, more personalized care.

- ■ Every touchpoint must be executed with thoughtfulness and precision.

I love this statement and couldn't agree with it more. Every touchpoint in healthcare at each stage—from healthy to sick to chronic to end-of-life and every point in between—should be executed with thoughtfulness and precision. To improve the health of individuals is our mission and that means shifting our focus to wellness, prevention, and value-based care. Imagine what would happen if we started thinking about touchpoints more granularly, mapping experiences and gaining insights from healthcare consumers themselves. I think we would gain clearer direction on how to improve the system, as well as identify new market opportunities for solving problems. We'd find a profusion of new ways to use the tools and technologies that we've discussed throughout the book, helping us to create a data-driven and connected health system.

■ ■ ■

Maintaining these foundations in creating products and services in healthcare can help shift our attention to consumer value and to thinking about healthcare as a total *experience* rather than sporadic touchpoints. In the last few years I've spent building new healthcare solutions the last few years building new healthcare solutions for SAS and for Remedy, a few things come to mind when I think about creating innovation in our new, data-filled health economy.

BUILD FOR HOW THE HEALTHCARE SYSTEM *SHOULD* WORK

Instead of trying to do our best in what is, let's break the mold by creating what could be. We can make bold changes and we can create exponential growth. That's why design thinking can really change the playing field for us in healthcare, helping us to create bottom-up innovation. We need to work with our larger goal in mind and continually ask ourselves: *Is this going to improve the health of individuals? Is this going to improve our healthcare system?* There have been far too many solutions built just because they fit in our current environment and current business models; they sometimes align with temporary needs, and sometimes they fail altogether. Whether it's a simple mobile application we're building or a complex analytics initiative, the reality is that if it doesn't meet the desires of our end-users it's not going to be successful. And whether our end-users are consumers or providers or health plans, we need to start with gaining *insights,* not making assumptions, to provide us the knowledge of our end-users' needs. These insights will help us learn how the system should work. Let's start with understanding the needs of the healthcare system and be bold in building for how healthcare *should* work.

RETHINK WORKFLOWS AND EXPERIENCES

Let's put experience innovation at the core of what we do and identify the most effective and efficient ways of doing things. If we analyze how people go through experiences, understand their stories, their behaviors, and their desires, we can craft more appropriate solutions that will truly make an impact on better health. Tools like experience blueprints will help us with understanding consumer experiences and provider workflows and in understanding consumer behavior. This builds on the understanding of our end-user needs and gives us more knowledge into bottlenecks and disruptions in workflows and experiences.

Look back at the example I gave in Chapter 3 about Kohl's (p. 33). Kohl's was able to take multiple customer touchpoints and create a seamless experience that connected various channels, like the Internet and the physical store. When these touchpoints are connected and the related information is connected, the experience becomes seamless. The result is that the customer is more satisfied, there are fewer barriers in purchasing, and the customer is more likely to purchase. And what's more, as we discussed in the Kohl's example, is the in-store experience actually becomes much more valuable to the shoppers because of the integration of their online activity. The human element isn't lost, but rather magnified with these digital channels and technologies. Even with other industries, like banking, we see that although customers are using multiple channels now, they're expecting (and receiving) higher value from their experience in person. They're more engaged through mobile banking and applications like Mint. Many of us haven't set foot in a bank in years, but feel more empowered than ever in managing our fiscal health. If done right in healthcare, the unwarranted ideas about doctors being replaced by technology and about losing the human relationship to digital health are actually quite the opposite of what will actually happen. This empowerment, part of the patient revolution, can bring trust, accountability, better collaboration, and more engagement. But first we have to adapt to modern needs and create value both inside *and* outside of the four walls of a doctor's office.

■ ■ ■

That's why we have to think about healthcare as two- dimensional: as both *health* and *care*. When I hear people talk about "the patient journey" and "the patient experience," it's typically about what patients experience within the confines of a hospital or a doctor's office. Sometimes, pre- and post-activities are touched on, like waiting rooms and checking out, but all of these activities deal with how we *care* for patients during their encounters with the system. As we identified early on, though, it's the totality of *health* that we need to address, and the *total* experience for consumers. Remember the example of hospitality that we discussed? In today's experience economy, hotel stayers may be checking into their rooms early through mobile apps, preordering television programs and snacks, and receiving personalized recommendations of places to eat near the hotel. And after the stay, they might receive promotions and offers catering to their preferences. It's a continuous relationship that keeps customers actively participating. Similarly, we want to focus on the total experience for healthcare consumers, extending the range of the experience to include daily activities that are not directly related to a healthcare engagement. After all, with 80 percent of health being dependent on factors outside of the care system, and with personal decisions being the most important factor in health, our mission of improving health for each individual can't possibly be addressed by optimizing only a small part of the patient journey.

DEVELOP THINGS THAT WORK TOGETHER

This is sort of an extension of the previous two sections, and it's critical to all the topics we've discussed throughout the book. We've talked about everything from the Internet of Things, to analytics frameworks, to health clouds and interoperability and ultimate connectivity. In sum, we need to build things that function together and are compatible with each other. As I've mentioned, many solutions are built just because they fit into our current environment and current business models. They sometimes align with temporary needs, and sometimes they fail altogether. They fail for a few different reasons: because their use becomes irrelevant in the fast-changing industry and they aren't built for future needs; the solution isn't designed with end-users in mind and therefore nobody uses it; the solution doesn't fit into existing workflows and experiences; or a combination of some or all of these. Often, brilliant ideas and innovations are unsuccessful even if the functionality of the product or service is exceptional.

The expectations of healthcare providers to adopt and use new technologies are unrealistic, impractical, and idealistic, if the new technologies don't fit seamlessly into their world of care. Integrating, for example, point-of-care analytics into EHR systems is critical. We can't expect providers to log into other portals and devices when already adopting EHR systems can be plenty tedious. Patient profiles and dashboards within EHR systems that give providers easy access and ease-of-use with point-of-care technologies will help adoption drastically. The same holds true on the consumer side, and usability and compatibility across devices—whether a wearable, a smartphone, or a tablet—need to exist to ensure active participation.

■ ■ ■

My team and I thought about this a lot when we were building Remedy. We wanted to make it simple, easy, and seamless, be it a 70-year-old or an 18-year-old using the application. By starting with the end-users, both consumers and providers, and determining how the tool *should* work and how it would fit into existing experiences and workflows, we were able to create something that users love.

At the end of the day, everything we create needs to be usable and make our lives easier, not more complex. This requires cooperation by multiple industries with healthcare organizations, including EHR companies, analytics companies, the cornucopia of digital health companies, and many others. The emergence of things like open APIs (application program interfaces), analytics frameworks, and mobile point-of-care tools is taking the industry much closer to the long-awaited connected system we're striving for. The more we can continue to build multidevice, multilevel functionality and compatibility, the more we'll find healthcare working like an actual system.

CLOSE THE LOOP

Information needs to be brought back full circle to the user, whoever the user may be. That means a learning health system that improves the more we use it, feedback on outcomes, going from tracking to guiding to improving health, and much more. On both the consumer and provider sides, we can leverage the constant hyperconnectivity that exists today to the vast array of networks and devices. Tools and technologies that apply analytics that provide real-time feedback, alert parties when issues arise, and provide recommendations and guidance, are all ways to create more accountability and improvement across the ecosystem of health and care.

FINAL THOUGHTS

I started working in the field of health analytics seven years ago, and in just seven years I've seen the industry transform and grow dramatically. Analytics in healthcare has expeditiously gone from a buzzword to a reality, and the demand to be more consumer-centric has been a driving force behind its adoption. It's been refreshing to see the industry pick up so much momentum in technology and innovation.

My hope is that we continue to head toward giving consumers the authority to engage the system in new ways, and that we focus on creating deeper and more meaningful experiences that invite consumers to participate. I hope that with novel tools, we improve disease management and that disease prevention becomes the norm, with clinicians and consumers tackling chronic conditions like diabetes and hypertension before they even start, and that we build cutting-edge technologies to advance clinical research and give consumers accurate and personalized diagnoses—the first time, every time. I want to see a system in which our electronic health records are owned by consumers, available to them at all times, and available to any place of care that they choose for them to be, where consumers are actively engaging in their treatment plans, and where consumers and clinicians are working in partnership to change deeply ingrained unhealthy behaviors and create new, healthy behaviors. With new activities and behaviors that are seamlessly integrated into daily lives, we'll cumulatively and over time start to make a big difference in the health of our nation.

Certainly, reinventing the system to reach these goals is no simple task. It'll take system-wide innovation and the participation of everyone in the industry. After all, the whole is greater than the sum of its parts, and it's the sustained effort across the entire system to commit to consumer-centric healthcare that will lead us there. This is only the beginning of the patient revolution, but we're off to a promising start.

NOTES

1. http://www.wsj.com/articles/innovation-is-sweeping-through-u-s-medical-schools-1424145650.
2. http://www.wsj.com/articles/innovation-is-sweeping-through-u-s-medical-schools-1424145650.

APPENDIX

Chapter Summaries

PART 1: THINK

The first part of the book is about changing the way we think about healthcare. By focusing on personal experiences and on human needs, I create a vision for the ideal healthcare system.

Chapter 1: Introduction

Chapter 1 begins with an introduction to design thinking and the experience economy—two foundational concepts that are central to the book. I was inspired to bring these concepts into healthcare after reading Tim Brown's book *Change by Design*, in which Brown discusses the elements of design thinking and experience innovation across products, services, and systems. I used the design thinking process as a framework for this book.

Design thinking is a human-centered approach to innovation that translates observations into insights and insights into products and services that improve lives. It's a unique process because it gets people involved from the very beginning and makes human needs central to each step of innovation. The process looks like this:

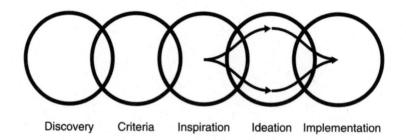

Discovery　　Criteria　　Inspiration　　Ideation　Implementation

My team and I at Remedy—a start-up focused on pain management—used design thinking to get our product off the ground, and I share a brief story about how we got started. We began by thoroughly understanding the needs and the *experience*s of pain patients and providers, something we don't do as often as we should in healthcare.

Today's world has been characterized as the *experience economy*, in which people shift from passive consumption to active participation.

Services across most industries have fully shifted toward delivering experiences, and most have gone beyond that to provide personalized and customized experiences. Whether we're sitting on an airplane, shopping for groceries, or checking into a hotel, we aren't just carrying out a function; we are having an *experience*. Moreover, we're active participators rather than passive consumers.

Design thinking helps us to create this active participation and better and more *total* experiences. In healthcare, not only do we need active participators and richer experiences, but with the industry becoming more patient-centric and value-based we need human-centered approaches that let us see healthcare through a different lens.

Chapter 2: Insight

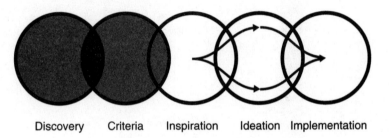

Discovery   Criteria   Inspiration   Ideation Implementation

The first stage of design thinking is the discovery stage, in which we gain insight into people's needs and desires. I went on a journey to find meaning behind *patient-centric* from patients themselves and I talk about all of the insights I found regarding individuals' healthcare experiences. My goal was to spark dialogue around what our typical and desired experiences really are. I had taken this approach with Remedy, and just as I had done for pain experiences, I wanted to learn about challenges and problem areas across the broader healthcare system. I found many consistent themes throughout everyone's experiences and also that there are a lot of opportunities to impact *health* and not just care.

Here's a glimpse of what I found:

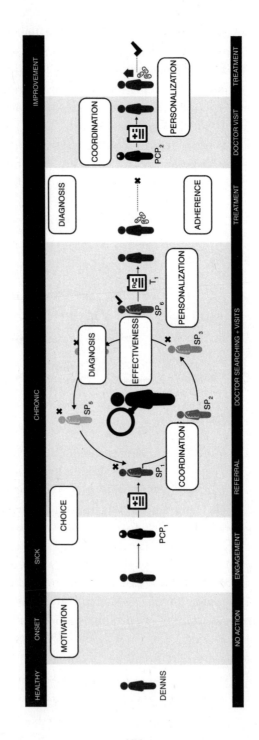

This is part of an experience blueprint that I created. (See Chapter 2, page 21 (BP of dennis's experience) for the entire blueprint.) An experience blueprint is a design thinking tool that lets you identify the most meaningful points or the biggest challenges from the customer's perspective (or in this case, the patient's). These points can then be turned into opportunities, which begin by identifying criteria—the second stage of design thinking. Here are the criteria I came up with:

- *How might we* encourage individuals to be more *motivated* in achieving better health?
- *How might we* ensure patient *adherence* to treatment plans?
- *How might we* create more opportunities for *choice* within the healthcare system?
- *How might we* improve the *coordination* of care among healthcare providers?
- *How might we* increase the *effectiveness* of healthcare services?
- *How might we* increase the accuracy and timeliness of medical *diagnostics*?
- *How might we* create more *personalization* of care?

Chapter 3: Inspiration

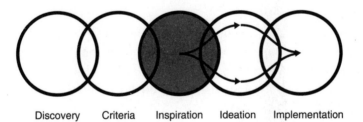

Discovery   Criteria   Inspiration   Ideation   Implementation

Inspiration is the next stage of design thinking, and in this chapter I look at other industries that have addressed similar issues as the ones I identified in my criteria. Specifically, I look at the banking and retail industries, as well as some forward-thinkers in healthcare.

Here's what I found:

- *Banking:* Banks are creating micro-segments of customers that help them to understand their customers at a more granular level. Many banks have embraced something called *customer experience management* (CEM), which is all about delivering personalized, contextual interactions that guide customers with their daily financial needs. CEM helps anticipate customer needs and enables real-time delivery of products at the right time, to the right people.

■ *Retail:* Retailers are creating personalization from many different angles and generating seamless experiences for their customers across various channels. For example, they're providing real-time personalized offers in stores through smartphones, bridging the mobile and in-store shopping experiences. They've also gone from sending blanket promotions to sending targeted offers based on individual shopper purchases, going as far as to predict what you might buy in your next visit to the store. And like banking, mobile shopping is becoming easier and more customized; personalized fashion experts, one-click-to-buy features, and customized fashion feeds are all part of the new shopping experience.

Both the banking and retail industries are already doing many of the things that we're striving for in healthcare. And they're doing it all through the use of data. It's their use of big data and analytics that's helping them, and other industries, to be successful in today's experience economy.

There's abundant opportunity for healthcare, too, in the experience economy. While we're still catching up, the industry is beginning to create a new patient experience through data-driven decision making. Both the banking and retail world are great sources of inspiration for how we might get there.

Chapter 4: Ideation

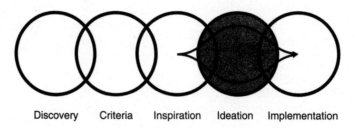

Discovery   Criteria   Inspiration   Ideation   Implementation

The ideation stage is my favorite part of the design thinking process. In this stage we combine the understanding we have of the problem space and the people we're designing for with our imaginations to generate solution concepts. So, taking the inspiration I gained from Chapter 3, what I identified in our criteria, and what I learned about patient desires, I asked myself what the ideal healthcare system might look like.

I introduce a lot of new ideas here, centered around a shift in authority from clinicians to patients. In a newly designed system, the role of the patient undergoes a revolution, moving from less of a patient to more of a *consumer* of healthcare. The focus of the system is far beyond sickness—it's about wellness and optimizing health, and about creating a *total* healthcare experience rather than a few sporadic points within the system.

I discuss the concept of health clouds and personal health clouds, which are large virtual stores where health data is stored, analyzed, and shared from. The cloud receives data that individuals generate, that their clinicians generate, and others, like their insurance companies, generate. But most important, the data created by the individual, either passively or actively, is what makes each health cloud unique. It gives people the freedom to include data that's relevant to their lifestyle and needs. For example, my health cloud may include information such as my meals, my yoga schedule and the calories burned in each class, my sleep schedule, my travel schedule, and other things. (See the next illustration.) It lets me pick what I want to include and ultimately looks at all of this information to find patterns and trends.

Personal health clouds are part of larger health clouds that capture information to help our entire healthcare system. Individuals can choose to anonymously participate in these big data clouds, and by gathering information from billions of individuals, everyone from researchers to clinicians to patients benefits. It automatically mines all of the data, reduces it into digestible tidbits really fast, and spits out information that clinicians and others can use for treating patients and for advancing medical knowledge.

PART 2: DO

Part 2 is about making our ideas a reality. It's about implementing change through novel tools and technologies, and identifying what's necessary for radical innovation in healthcare.

Chapter 5: Implementation Part 1

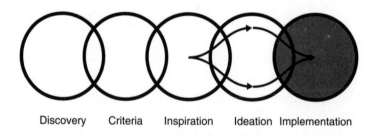

Discovery   Criteria   Inspiration   Ideation   Implementation

Chapters 5 through 7 cover the implementation stage, where I discuss how we can implement the ideas that we've generated thus far in the book. Chapter 5 kicks off the discussion with the tools and technologies that can help us in creating an improved system. I talk in detail about the different types of health data and analytics methods, as well as trends that are impacting the growth of data and analytics.

The amount of healthcare data is rapidly growing, and sources like claims, electronic health records, and mobile applications are feeding the big data revolution. All of this data introduces new opportunities for us to get a complete picture of the healthcare system and understand in detail the interdependencies that drive health outcomes. It also can help us to understand the factors *outside* of the healthcare system that impact health, like behaviors, education, and our environments. These are critical, as they make up 80 percent of the total factors that impact health.

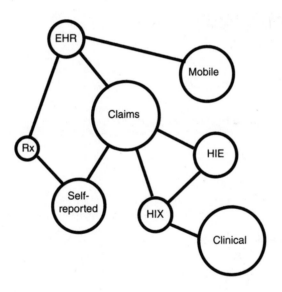

When we bring all of this data together, the opportunities for us to analyze these rich stores of information are virtually infinite. And now, with the explosion of digitization and trends like the Internet of Things and machine learning, big data analytics is critical to a modern healthcare system.

Here's an example of a maturity model with descriptive, predictive, and prescriptive analytics. I take you through it in depth in the chapter.

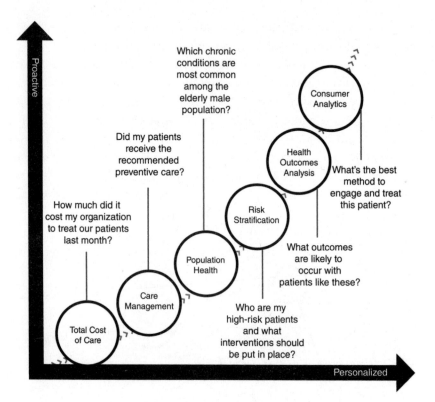

Chapter 6: Implementation Part 2

In this chapter, I continue the discussion on implementation and discuss how we can use big data and analytics to address the first three criteria.

1. *How might we* encourage individuals to be more *motivated* in achieving better health?

2. *How might we* ensure patient *adherence* to treatment plans?

3. *How might we* create more opportunities for *choice* within the healthcare system?

To address motivation and adherence, I talk about applications that payers and providers can use, as well as consumer applications, that will help create behavior change. Sustained behavior change is critical to improving health, as detrimental behaviors like poor diet, not adhering to prescribed medications, and smoking not only have negative impacts on long-term health but also cost the healthcare system a fortune.

For payers and providers, I discuss population health analytics to help provide ongoing support to individuals outside the clinical setting. Population health is about identifying those patients who have care gaps and would benefit most from additional support. It's also about providing targeted outreach to specific patients at the optimal time, which leverages behavioral analytics.

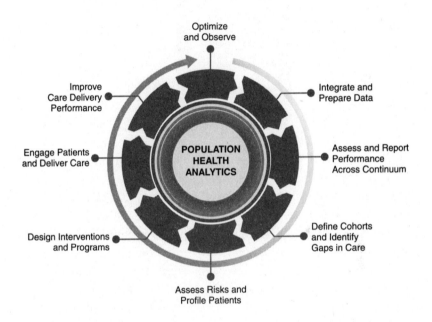

Behavioral analytics helps provide personalized guidance for consumers and is extremely valuable to both businesses and consumers. For healthcare consumers, behavioral analytics can help us create personalization by going from tracking to guiding.

In today's digital age we're tracking everything, from what we eat to the number of calories burned, to the distance we've traveled. Our social networks are even involved to garner encouragement and support. However, tracking systems are most helpful for those individuals who've already established a behavior, not for those who want to adopt a new habit or behavior. In order to achieve long-term behavior change, we need to think about taking tracking to the next level. What we really need to know is how far we *should* walk, or what we *should* eat. This is the leap from tracking to *guiding* behavior that I talk about in this chapter.

The last part of the chapter is about creating consumer choice and transparency throughout the system. I talk about a state government initiative called the all-payer claims database (APCD) as a platform for innovation. APCDs are repositories that collect healthcare claims data from all healthcare payers in a state, including both private and public payers. It provides a foundation to offer price and quality transparency to consumers, promoting choice and more retail-like healthcare. In addition, it has the potential to drive cost containment and quality improvement efforts across many different aspects of healthcare. I discuss in detail the APCD landscape, the possibilities for innovation, and some best practices for creating an APCD in the chapter.

Chapter 7: Implementation Part 3

Chapter 7 is about how we might address the remaining criteria. This is the most technical chapter in the book, and I go into detail about various analytics applications and show some reports I created using SAS Visual Analytics.

I start with addressing the next two criteria, coordination and effectiveness:

4. *How might we* improve the *coordination* of care among healthcare providers?

5. *How might we* increase the *effectiveness* of healthcare services?

Improving the coordination and effectiveness of care involves changing our volume-based system. Making the shift from volume to value,
however, is complex and requires new ways to analyze data. That's
why we need episode analytics to help us balance quality and costs,
create better coordination of care among providers, and improve the
effectiveness of services.

Episode analytics is an advanced method of looking at episodes
of care. Episodes of care are basically bundles of various services that
make up a certain episode, such as a knee replacement. Instead of
accounting for just the procedure itself, an episode of care involves
the *entire* path of care for the knee replacement service. I dive into this
topic in detail and show you how an episode of care is constructed.
I also discuss the various analytics use cases that are made possible
by creating these episodes. They give us the ability to do things like
see a holistic view of a patient, identify potentially avoidable costs
and treatments, and measure the variation in care across different
providers. Plus, predictive analytics, like forecasting and trending,
can be done to understand the potential gains in shared savings
models, helping providers to remain profitable while offering the best
possible care.

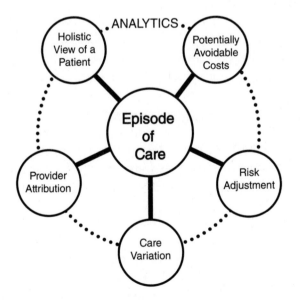

The second part of the chapter is about generating more accurate diagnoses and more personalization, the final two criteria:

6. *How might we* increase the accuracy and timeliness of medical *diagnostics?*

7. *How might we* create more *personalization* of care?

This section is one of my favorite parts of the book, as it highlights just how impactful big data and analytics can be in healthcare. Through machine learning and artificial intelligence (AI) we have the potential to create personalization by dramatically improving medical diagnostics and treatments. Without any human intervention, computers can provide individuals with accurate, usable information that could potentially save lives.

We'll see machine learning and AI become extremely ground-breaking in healthcare. Think about the billions (trillions, gazillions) of data points that could potentially be gathered with all of the healthcare data that's out there—claims, EHRs, labs, imaging, mobile health, social media, and even genome data. Machine learning could be so powerful that it would find patterns in all of this unimaginable data, and by using an individual's genomic structure, tell us what treatment would work best for that person. And with natural language processing (NLP) and machine learning in conjunction we could see services like a Siri for healthcare that translates everyday words into diagnoses. One day, NPL could even become so accurate that it would capture individual sentiments. In fact, it's already so advanced that it can capture subtleties, nuances, and idioms in our language. What if, instead of waiting for your doctor's appointment, you told your phone the details of how you're feeling, and it took that information, along with all the other data from your personal health cloud, to provide you a diagnosis and treatment plan, all in a matter of seconds? Imagine what advancements like these could do for the access to healthcare.

Chapter 8: Innovation

Chapter 8 takes you through everything we've discussed—insights, ideation, inspiration, and implementation—and puts a wrapper around it. I visit the topics of human-centered design and design thinking in more depth, and also talk about exponential growth in healthcare.

Dr. Peter Diamandis utilizes a framework of six *D*s to think about exponential growth processes in technology. He characterizes these processes as digitization, deception, disruption, dematerialization, demonetization, and democratization. I look at health analytics broadly and apply these six *D*s to think about where we are with radical growth in the field. I conclude that *modernization* sums up everything I've discussed throughout the book.

Motivation Adherence	❯	Population Health Behavioral Analytics Behavior Change Platforms
Choice	❯	Data Transparency All-Payer Claims Databases Personalized Health Plans
Coordination Effectiveness	❯	Episode Analytics Potentially Avoidable Costs Holistic View of Patient
Diagnosis Personalization	❯	Machine Learning Artificial Intelligence Natural Language Processing

Modernization is the *process of adapting to modern needs or habits, typically by installing modern equipment or adopting modern ideas or methods*. I break down this definition as it relates to healthcare.

- *Adapting to modern needs or habits:* In order to adapt to modern-day consumer needs and habits, we must change the way we approach healthcare. Considering consumers' desires, their environment, their lifestyle, and the way they engage with other services in the experience economy will help us create a new health economy that integrates into our daily lives.

- *Adopting modern ideas or methods:* Modern ideas and methods in healthcare is everything from novel data analytics strategies and data-driven decision making to new methods of payment or delivery in healthcare. It also applies to new ways of thinking about innovation and problem solving, like design thinking and the six *D*s of exponential growth.

- *Installing modern equipment:* This piece is all about your technology infrastructure. Do you have the right platforms in place to create optimal value to consumers? Do you have access to the right data? Are you able to handle large amounts of data? Are you using your data to its potential? It's also about adapting to new consumer technologies, whether it's a smartphone, a wearable device, or integrating into the Internet of Things.

I close the chapter with how to achieve modernization. Interoperability is the key topic here. For solutions to work together, for data to work together, for the healthcare *system* to work together, we need interoperability. Interoperability in healthcare faces a lot of cultural, technological, and regulatory barriers, but we're making a lot of progress despite those, all of which I highlight in this chapter.

Chapter 9: Individual

The final chapter of the book brings my focus back to the individual. How do we move forward with all of these new tools, technologies, and methods to truly reach our goal of improving health for each individual?

Three guidelines offered by Tim Brown resonated with me as I wrote this last chapter. Brown relates these guidelines to successful experience brands, not systems or services, but I think they're all relevant to healthcare. The three guidelines are:

1. A successful experience requires active consumer participation.
2. A customer experience that feels authentic, genuine, and compelling is likely to be delivered by employees operating within an experience culture themselves.
3. Every touchpoint must be executed with thoughtfulness and precision.

I couldn't agree with these guidelines more. As we embrace a new health economy and modernize the system, each of these guidelines is very relevant across the industry. Maintaining these foundations in creating healthcare products and services can help shift our attention to consumer value and to thinking about healthcare as a total experience rather than sporadic touchpoints.

Having spent the last few years building new healthcare solutions for SAS and for Remedy, a few things come to mind when I think about creating innovation in our new, data-filled health economy. I elaborate on some of my own guidelines for creating new healthcare products and services, such as building for how the healthcare system *should* work, rethinking workflows and experiences, developing things that work together, and closing the loop.

My closing thoughts are focused on my hopes that we continue to head toward giving consumers the authority to engage the system in new ways; that we focus on creating deeper and more meaningful experiences that invite consumers to participate; that wellness and prevention become the norm; that consumers are actively engaging in their treatment plans; that consumers and clinicians are working in partnership to change deeply ingrained unhealthy behaviors, and create new, healthy behaviors. With new activities and behaviors that are seamlessly integrated into daily lives, we'll cumulatively and over time make a big difference in the health of our nation.

Index

Note: Page references followed by *f* and *t* indicate an illustrated figure and table, respectively.

190 ▶INDEX

as one of six Ds of exponential
growth, 145, 183
Dignity Health, 90
discovery, as first step of design
thinking process, 17–24,
17*f*, 142, 170*f*, 171*f*
disruption, as one of six Ds
of exponential growth,
146, 183
Dixon, Pam, 91
DXLab, 5

E
EDW (enterprise data
warehouse), 67–70, 68*f*
effectiveness, as criteria in
design thinking process,
25–26, 142–143, 150*f*,
180–181, 183
electronic health records (EHRs),
11–12, 56, 152–153
electronic medical records
(EMRs), 11–12, 56
empathy, 6, 142
employers, APCD and, 105*t*
Engage Patients & Coordinate
Care, as step in Population
Health Wheel, 89, 89*f*, 179*f*
Enlitic, 138, 139
enterprise data warehouse
(EDW), 67–70, 68*f*
episode analytics, 121–122,
181, 181*f*
episode of care,
about, 123–124
calculating cost of, 124–125
constructing an, 122–123,
122*f*, 124*f*
equipment, modern, 151, 184
experience,
rethinking, 163–165
as a teacher, 7–10

experience blueprint,
about, 17–20, 86–87, 142,
172*f*, 173
of Dennis's story, 21*f*, 27*f*
experience economy, 8–10,
170–171
exponential growth, 145–148

F
Facebook, 139
feasibility,
as a lens of design thinking,
52–55, 53*f*, 142
of technology, 53–55, 53*f*
"fee-for-service" model, 10
FitBit, 44, 91, 93
Fogg, B.J., 94–96, 160
Foundation for a Healthy
Kentucky, 103

G
Geneia, 90
Gilmore, James, 8–10
Ginger.io, 76
GlaxoSmithKline, 99, 113
Gold, Stephen, 59
Google, 135
growth, exponential, 145–148
guiding behavior, 94–96, 179

H
Hadoop, 36, 54, 63, 66–70,
68*f*, 69*f*, 146
HCAHPS (Hospital Consumer
Assessment of Healthcare
Providers and Systems), 57
HCCI (Health Care Cost
Institute), 99
health analytics,
framework of, 149*f*
as a trend impacting advanced
analytics, 70
Health Analytics (Burke), 70

Triple Aim, 98
Trunk, 33
Turntable Health, 34

V
Validic, 154
value, delivering to consumers,
110–111
value-based care, 10–11,
118–119, 130–139, 181
viability, as a lens of design
thinking, 52, 53*f*, 142

visual analytics, 64, 79, 180
volume-based care, 10–11,
118–119, 181

W
Washington, 103
web portals, 112–113
workflows, rethinking,
163–165

X
Xing, Eric, 135

Wiley & SAS Business Series

The Wiley & SAS Business Series presents books that help senior-level managers with their critical management decisions.

Titles in the Wiley & SAS Business Series include:

Agile by Design: An Implementation Guide to Analytic Lifecycle Management by Rachel Alt-Simmons

Analytics in a Big Data World: The Essential Guide to Data Science and Its Applications by Bart Baesens

Bank Fraud: Using Technology to Combat Losses by Revathi Subramanian

Big Data Analytics: Turning Big Data into Big Money by Frank Ohlhorst

Big Data, Big Innovation: Enabling Competitive Differentiation through Business Analytics by Evan Stubbs

Business Analytics for Customer Intelligence by Gert Laursen

Business Intelligence Applied: Implementing an Effective Information and Communications Technology Infrastructure by Michael Gendron

Business Intelligence and the Cloud: Strategic Implementation Guide by Michael S. Gendron

Business Transformation: A Roadmap for Maximizing Organizational Insights by Aiman Zeid

Connecting Organizational Silos: Taking Knowledge Flow Management to the Next Level with Social Media by Frank Leistner

Data-Driven Healthcare: How Analytics and BI Are Transforming the Industry by Laura Madsen

Delivering Business Analytics: Practical Guidelines for Best Practice by Evan Stubbs

Demand-Driven Forecasting: A Structured Approach to Forecasting, Second Edition by Charles Chase

Demand-Driven Inventory Optimization and Replenishment: Creating a More Efficient Supply Chain by Robert A. Davis

Developing Human Capital: Using Analytics to Plan and Optimize Your Learning and Development Investments by Gene Pease, Barbara Beresford, and Lew Walker

The Executive's Guide to Enterprise Social Media Strategy: How Social Networks Are Radically Transforming Your Business by David Thomas and Mike Barlow

Economic and Business Forecasting: Analyzing and Interpreting Econometric Results by John Silvia, Azhar Iqbal, Kaylyn Swankoski, Sarah Watt, and Sam Bullard

Financial Institution Advantage and the Optimization of Information Processing by Sean C. Keenan

Financial Risk Management: Applications in Market, Credit, Asset, and Liability Management and Firmwide Risk by Jimmy Skoglund and Wei Chen

Foreign Currency Financial Reporting from Euros to Yen to Yuan: A Guide to Fundamental Concepts and Practical Applications by Robert Rowan

Fraud Analytics Using Descriptive, Predictive, and Social Network Techniques: A Guide to Data Science for Fraud Detection by Bart Baesens, Veronique Van Vlasselaer, and Wouter Verbeke

Harness Oil and Gas Big Data with Analytics: Optimize Exploration and Production with Data Driven Models by Keith Holdaway

Health Analytics: Gaining the Insights to Transform Health Care by Jason Burke

Heuristics in Analytics: A Practical Perspective of What Influences Our Analytical World by Carlos Andre, Reis Pinheiro, and Fiona McNeill

Hotel Pricing in a Social World: Driving Value in the Digital Economy by Kelly McGuire

Human Capital Analytics: How to Harness the Potential of Your Organization's Greatest Asset by Gene Pease, Boyce Byerly, and Jac Fitz-enz

Implement, Improve and Expand Your Statewide Longitudinal Data System: Creating a Culture of Data in Education by Jamie McQuiggan and Armistead Sapp

Killer Analytics: Top 20 Metrics Missing from your Balance Sheet by Mark Brown

Mobile Learning: A Handbook for Developers, Educators, and Learners by Scott McQuiggan, Lucy Kosturko, Jamie McQuiggan, and Jennifer Sabourin

The Patient Revolution: How Big Data and Analytics Are Transforming the Healthcare Experience by Krisa Tailor

Predictive Analytics for Human Resources by Jac Fitz-enz and John Mattox II

Predictive Business Analytics: Forward-Looking Capabilities to Improve Business Performance by Lawrence Maisel and Gary Cokins

Retail Analytics: The Secret Weapon by Emmett Cox

Social Network Analysis in Telecommunications by Carlos Andre Reis Pinheiro

Statistical Thinking: Improving Business Performance, Second Edition by Roger W. Hoerl and Ronald D. Snee

Taming the Big Data Tidal Wave: Finding Opportunities in Huge Data Streams with Advanced Analytics by Bill Franks

Too Big to Ignore: The Business Case for Big Data by Phil Simon

The Value of Business Analytics: Identifying the Path to Profitability by Evan Stubbs

The Visual Organization: Data Visualization, Big Data, and the Quest for Better Decisions by Phil Simon

Trade-Based Money Laundering: The Next Frontier in International Money Laundering Enforcement by John Cassara

Understanding the Predictive Analytics Lifecycle by Al Cordoba

Unleashing Your Inner Leader: An Executive Coach Tells All by Vickie Bevenour

Using Big Data Analytics: Turning Big Data into Big Money by Jared Dean

Visual Six Sigma, Second Edition by Ian Cox, Marie Gaudard, Philip Ramsey, Mia Stephens, and Leo Wright

Win with Advanced Business Analytics: Creating Business Value from Your Data by Jean Paul Isson and Jesse Harriott

For more information on any of the above titles, please visit www.wiley.com.